More Praise for BEYOND THE WHITENESS OF WHITENESS:

"A beautifully written, deeply thoughtful journey into the worlds of self and other." — *Kirkus Reviews*

"Lazarre's voice is artful and measured [and provides] substantial food for thought for both white and black perspectives on the murky issue of race in America." — *Publisher's Weekly*

"Lazarre cuts close to the bone in this penetrating 'story of the education of an American woman.'" — MARY CARROLL, *Booklist*

"[Lazarre]. . . moves the reader. . . . When she writes, 'I wish I could become Black for my sons,' she delves straight into the heart of her dilemma." — HELEN SCHULMAN, *Elle*

"Powerful, moving, and beautifully written. . ." — RICHARD L. ZWEIGENHAFT, *Greensboro News & Record*

"*Beyond the Whiteness of Whiteness* will be the classic Lazarre's *The Mother Knot* has become, a book in which a piece of American experience gets its full telling, a necessary book." — ANN SNITOW, the New School for Social Research

"In the end there is the great gift of being taken into the life of American black culture. On the way there, this mother and child — the most intimate of relationships from infancy — has no public or political recognition for years. A kind of love story and useful as well to people in interracial lives and families." — GRACE PALEY

"Through the profoundly human caring of this book; its luminous beauty, passionate authenticity, truth and power; its multi-lensed and sourced hard-wrung wisdom — and yes, through the art with which it is written — we see, feel, understand what we never have before, the ways of the Whiteness of Whiteness; and we are challenged, enlarged, and enabled, as was Jane Lazarre, to move Beyond." — TILLIE OLSEN

BEYOND THE WHITENESS

OF WHITENESS

Memoir of a White Mother of Black Sons

Jane Lazarre

DUKE UNIVERSITY PRESS   Durham and London 1996

First printing in paperback, 1997
© 1996 Duke University Press
All rights reserved
Printed in the United States of America
on acid-free paper ∞. Typeset in Galliard by
Keystone Typesetting, Inc.
Library of Congress Cataloging-in-
Publication Data appear on the last
printed page of this book.

For Douglas H. White
    Lois Meadows-White
    and
    Leona Ruggiero,
    who has been with me
    every step of the way.
And for
    Simeon Meadows White,
    in lasting memory.

CONTENTS

Acknowledgments   ix

Prologue   xiii

ONE. The Richmond Museum of the Confederacy   1

TWO. Color Blind: The Whiteness of Whiteness   21

THREE. Passing Over   53

FOUR. Reunions, Retellings, Refrains   99

FIVE. A Color with No Precise Name   125

Notes   137

ACKNOWLEDGMENTS

I received much help in the writing of this book. Most of the writers whose work has taught and inspired me are mentioned within the text, but there are other friends and colleagues whose support has been crucial to me in all stages of the writing.

Miriam Sivan, Ruth Charney, and Sara Ruddick were my earliest readers. I can never adequately acknowledge my appreciation for their intelligent response, their encouragement, and their love.

Maureen Reddy's book, *Crossing the Color Line,* about being the white Irish mother of Black children was an inspiration to me, and Maureen's early reading, suggestions, and strong support greatly aided the course of my own work.

During various stages of writing, I counted on trusted readers to help me evaluate, change, or remain confident in what I had written. These people—Donald Scott, Nancy Barnes, Claire Potter, Rachel Cowan, Connie Brown, Jan Clausen, Carol Ascher, Marnie Mueller, Lynda Schor, Carole Rosenthal, Edith Konecky, Rebecca Kavaler, Gary Lemons, Gregory Tewksbury, and my sister, Emily Lazarre—all made invaluable suggestions, thereby helping me to see things more clearly.

I owe very special thanks to Sekou Sundiata, whose reading of and response to the manuscript was crucial and detailed. As an artist and a human being, he inspires and points the way.

I am extremely grateful to Rachel Toor and Peter Guzzardi of Duke University Press for their enthusiasm and help with all the stages of publishing this book.

Words cannot fully express my gratitude and regard for my agent, Wendy Weil, and her assistant, Claire Needell. They not only provided the usual labor of agents, but kept me going during a crisis in the life of this book. If not for their faith, I could not have completed the work of bringing this memoir into the public realm.

Several years ago, while participating in a faculty seminar at the Eugene Lang College, I began to learn some of what I have tried to present here regarding the way in which all our knowledge of ourselves and our society is illuminated by a study of race and racism in a multicultural perspective. I am indebted to my student assistant, Cynthia Cohn, to my colleagues in that seminar, and especially to its leader and convener, Toni Oliviero, Associate Dean of the college, for expanding my knowledge of African American and Latino studies and of the profound relationships between curriculum and pedagogy.

I would like to thank the students in my seminars: "Writers Teaching Writing" and "African American Autobiography and Writing the Self." Their insights and explorations are threaded throughout the book.

At a later stage, Lindsay Feinberg, a talented and trusted student, gave generous help with research during a busy time.

This is a memoir of one woman, but it is also a story of a family. My family has supported me emotionally, intellectually, and spiritually at every stage of my writing.

Lois Meadows-White, my mother-in-law, has taught me much of what I know about the Black experience. Her stories have inspired me, and with great generosity she has witnessed some of them become my own stories to pass on. Her editing for accuracy of fact and rightness of tone was invaluable.

My husband, Douglas Hughes White, listened to and read every chapter, discussed every idea with me when I was uncertain or excited, and gave the unfailing support he has given to me and my work over many years. It is largely because of his belief in me that I had the temerity to write this story in the first place.

More than anyone else, I want to thank my sons, Adam Lazarre-White and Khary Lazarre-White. Through their example, their integrity in the search for self, their companionship, and the struggles we have been through together, I came to understand something about what is now being called the American racial divide. Even as they pointed out that treacherous geography, they provided the love and friendship which identify the crossing points and build the bridges we count on as we continue our lives in this nation which is so endangered by the racial conflict tearing at its soul.

PROLOGUE

It is the spring of 1995, and I am attending my younger son's graduation from college. A departmental ritual follows the enormous all-college ceremony, and it is here, in the relative intimacy of the smaller community of students and professors who have worked together for years, that students most deeply feel the dimensions of their accomplishment and the commencement of a new period in their lives. In a small theater housed in the Afro-American studies department, where my son Khary has pursued his academic major, studying African, African Caribbean, and African American history and literature, there is a feeling of both excitement and belonging as parents and relatives take their seats, a sense of coming home from the enormous and largely white world of the all-campus ceremony. Here, most of the people — professors, students, and families — are Black, although there are a few other whites besides myself, other mothers, fathers, aunts, cousins, and grandparents, whose families are Black. We stand out as our children stand out in the wider campus of Brown University, scattered faces "of color" in a vast sea of whiteness, the usual tiny minority of "diverse" Americans on campuses where racial balance has supposedly been achieved.

I am drenched by the rain which has been pouring down on us all morning, but I am comfortable in this lovely theater, still decorated by the set of the play performed the night before and so looking more like the large living room it represents than a formal hall. Five professors sit in a semicircle on the stage. The fifteen or twenty graduates sit on couches and chairs in front of them, then turn toward the chairman of the department, who rises to speak. My husband, Douglas, his mother Lois, and sister Sherrill, my sister Emily and her daughter Sarah, my son Adam, and one or two close friends touch each other's hands, glance at each other's moist eyes and proud expressions, as Khary and the other students listen to their faculty, some of whom have been more than teachers, have been true mentors and friends.

The talk to the graduates is about how exceptional they are, and about how exceptional they must continue to be. Here, in this familial setting, the traditional warning to Black youth is made again, unchanged for centuries: You are wonderful, yes. But you must always be better than white people, you must be exceptional in order to succeed in this society; you must be prepared for the battles ahead which will challenge your fortitude and strain your capacities to their limits; with all your distinguished fellowships and honors (and there are many which will soon be named) you must be prepared for the harsh world now, a world where the color of your skin is still a daily, pervasive constraint. But you all know that, the graduates are told, and you have overcome, and you will continue to overcome.

Professor Anani Dzidzienyo, Khary's beloved mentor, performs a traditional West African libation, a blessing from Ghana, his homeland. Next, from Lane College in Tennessee, a young gospel singer with a miraculous voice stands to perform the song we have listened to and sung during every Black event of the three-day weekend, the Black National Anthem, "Lift Every Voice and Sing." When he reaches the lines of the first verse, "Sing a song full of the pain that the dark past has taught us. Sing a song, full of the hope that the present has brought us," I begin to cry. I am crying because over many years of raising Black sons, living in a Black family, and studying and teaching African American literature, I have learned the truth now being talked and sung about, the truth of ongoing American racism that my children have always had to and will continue to have to struggle against. I am thinking of the thousands of white students and faculty in this liberal, Ivy League college who would be shocked if they heard the message being given, in 1995, to these Black graduates — still, the same message, accepted by faculty, students, and families as unquestionable truth. Though I have spent many years wrestling in myself with the "whiteness of whiteness" — that terrible and inexcusable ignorance of racism which denies history and reality — still, I can imagine the shock that would be felt by most white people were they sitting in this audience as I am.

But there is no shock registered in the reactions of the hundred or so family members who now burst into applause for the achievements of their sons and daughters. They take their turns walking onto the stage to receive their diplomas, their honors read aloud; they greet their teachers in this academic department that has been an intellectual and spiritual home to them during four often difficult years in a world where they have had to combat daily not only the realities of racism but the potentially mind-destroying insistence on its denial. Khary, back in his seat, is embraced on both sides by his friends while his brother Adam snaps the photos. I am crying still, not only with pride for my own son, but with pride for them all. And I am grateful that I no longer experience shock when listening to stories about the pervasive reality of American racism, but only the familiarity of recognition, of truth.

It was in 1979 and 1980, while teaching Women's Studies at the City College of New York, when Khary was only six and Adam ten, that I began to read widely and teach African American literature. As a writer and passionate reader of fiction and memoir, I discovered that African

American literature often described my own deepest emotions, present-ing a vision of the world and experience that was profoundly familiar to me, a white, Jewish woman.

Was this because I myself was what we now call a "first generation" col-lege student? Because I had been raised in the subculture of the American Left to understand that slavery and racism sit at the heart of American experience, a cruel mockery of the idea and practice of democracy? Was it because the classic and universal theme of suffering, resistance, and libera-tion finds such profound resonance in literature written by Americans who know that theme intimately, have experienced it in a thousand fam-ily and communal stories for 400 years? Or, was it because I have spent my adult life living in a Black family, raising Black sons, forming my most in-timate relationships with African Americans, learning their culture, shar-ing their sorrows, marveling at the capacity for survival and transforma-tion that characterizes this most influential of American "sub" cultures?

No doubt all of these aspects of my identity rendered me especially receptive to Black literature and culture. Yet, it was not until I witnessed a special museum exhibit about American slavery that I became fully conscious of a transformation that had been occurring in me over many years yet was still not precisely named. Then I began to understand in a new way my own miseducation as a white American, and the lifelong re-education in this matter of race Americans have to undergo if we are to cease — to use Toni Morrison's phrase — "playing in the dark."

This "matter of race" must include stories of whiteness. There are millions of these stories embedded in American experience, stories of hatred and of blindness, of virulent contempt, and ordinary ignorance, and also stories of the struggle to battle injustice through knowledge and activism. But understanding racism does not occur automatically or quickly, through an act of will or as a result of simple decency and hatred of prejudice. Racism involves power, an intricate pattern of privilege we enjoy as white Americans whether we are aware of it or not, whether we want it or not. And while I understand the dangers of a merely sentimen-tal guilt, I believe there is some burden we must bear by being white Americans. This is a burden which can be redemptive, not oppressive. It is a burden which involves joining, not exclusion. It reminds me of the first time I, as a young woman, was allowed to be a pallbearer, a responsibility usually reserved for men in a family. I remember feeling a sense of self-respect, of being honored by being allowed to help support the coffin of a beloved brother-in-law. I wanted the strained muscles and aching back I knew would follow the next morning, and when a fellow pallbearer, a man, offered to carry my load as well as his own, I responded, I'll do my share.

This book is part of my attempt to do my share. I was raised in a Jewish family which was by and large nonobservant while still valuing its Jewishness. My children have been close to their Jewish as well as to their Black family. They have attended yearly Seders and Hanukkah as well as Christmas celebrations. In our own unconventional and secular way, we celebrated their thirteenth birthdays as Bar Mitzvahs. For most of their growing up, Douglas and I defined our family as "biracial." But that is a term we now see as problematic — as if there were two neatly defined races; as if there were an indisputable entity called race; as if young men with brown skins can ever be considered "part white" in America; as if Adam, now an actor, can audition for "white" parts in film, TV, or most theater; as if Khary, a young Black man walking on the streets late at night, can expect to be treated by the police like a young white man because his mother is white. As with any other identity, how one experiences oneself in the everyday outside world must become internal as well, or the mind splits, even sanity may slip, imbalance threatens.

Adam and Khary, now fully grown, live in a world where race and racism confront them every day. They are young Black men who, like many other Black Americans, possess a mixture of cultural heritages, including a particular form of secular American Judaism, and a mixture of genetic inheritances making up who they are.

There is another part of my life that is pertinent to this story, another voice in this memoir. As a writer and teacher of writing for many years, I have been involved with the genre of autobiography. I have written personal essays, memoirs, and consciously used autobiography in a variety of ways in my fiction, especially in my last novel, *Worlds Beyond My Control.* I teach autobiographical writing to undergraduates, focusing on the rich tradition of African American autobiography as a reading curriculum. In the course of this work, I have come to appreciate an approach to autobiographical writing which includes storytelling, descriptive narrative, and the interpretive voice of the essay—all with the aim of seeing ever more broadly into one's own individual experience and thus forging a more authentic relation to the world. I believe that identity and the search for consciousness are profoundly linked to cultural meanings and the historical moment in which we live. And I believe that "writing the self" is, therefore, an act of faith in human connection. In my first memoir, *The Mother Knot,* I claimed what was to become a lifelong subject: the experience of motherhood and the many ways in which that experience reveals, sustains, and constantly recreates my sense of connection to and responsibility toward a wider world.

In all my work since then, and especially in this book, I have tried, in a way, to use memoir to transcend itself; not only to recall and describe experience but to understand its significance beyond the self. Indeed, the unnatural split between individual and historical consciousness, where the one seems to emerge and prevail wholly independent of the other, is part of a distorted vision resulting from privilege, part of an ideology of individualism fraught with false stories which are dangerous to personal as well as to political life. The link between an individual life story and the collective story which gives context to that life is a defining formal and thematic aspect of African American autobiography. It is to the great American literary tradition of Frederick Douglass and Harriet Jacobs, to Richard Wright, Langston Hughes, Maya Angelou, and Malcolm X, to Audre Lorde, to the contemporary writers bell hooks and Patricia Williams, to many many others, and especially to the great master of this form, James Baldwin, that I owe my understanding of the rich possibilities of a resonant genre which has so enabled me as a writer and a person.

In many ways, of course, my experience as a white mother of Black sons does not fit the accepted stereotypes of racial difference and conflict.

There is a way in which our relations are and always have been beyond race. There is a place, a kind of psychic location, where what the racially polarized world of America sees as "racial difference" disappears for us. Nevertheless, the rather innocent notion I maintained in the beginning of this journey — that racial tensions would stop outside the door of our home, outside the borders of our family life — is dispelled now. Race, racial identity, racism, and African American history and politics — all are recurring motifs in our separate identities as well as our joined family life.

All of my work as a writer, teacher, and student of African American literature, then, is "colored" by my particular experience, this central fact of my life, this privilege, as I see it, of experiencing motherhood and coming to full adulthood in a culture very different from my own. It is equally true that my experience of motherhood has been dramatically affected in the past years by reading and thinking about what it means, how it feels to be an African American living in the United States only four generations after the end of slavery, the *first* generation not raised in the American form of apartheid known as "segregation" or "Jim Crow."

This is a memoir, then, told in many voices — the voice of the mother, of the teacher, of the Jewish woman, daughter of immigrants and American radicals; it also includes the voice of the wife of twenty-seven years of an African American man. Ironically, race has never been an issue in our marital life. We have never had a fight in which race was a conflict between us, although we have had countless arguments and discussions concerning matters of race. I am not certain why this is, in the same sense that no single thread can ever be neatly isolated from the fabric of a long-standing marriage. Perhaps we were both outsiders of a sort who didn't mind that position as much as some others. Certainly, the support and love of both our families has sustained us and our children over the years. I am an eager learner who likes to listen to other people's stories as much as I like to tell and retell my own, and the theme of liberation of peoples and the self has been a defining one in my psychological and intellectual life. And there was so much to learn about African American history and culture, a limitless enrichment of language, art, politics, and perspective

I became aware of and intrigued by from the first months of my belonging to a Black American family. As for Douglas, he too is attracted to difference, has always been drawn in particular to certain aspects of Jewish cultural and personal life; and he is above all a patient man. Although the expectation that he will continually and repeatedly educate any and all white people who come his way into the realities of American racism can be as much a strain on him as it is on any other Black person, no explanation or opportunity to educate the white people he loves has ever seemed a burden to him. This is a virtue one has no right to expect in everyone one meets, yet it is probably the central virtue that enabled our deepening connection over so many years.

This journey, however, has not been an easy or simple one for me. And perhaps reading the coming pages will not always be easy for the white reader, even the white reader who loves liberty, the white "fellow traveler" in the fight against American racism who bears her burden willingly and gratefully. It would be presumptuous to offer a simple solution or a neat linear record ending in perfect transcendence. It has been a long journey, and it is still going on, an incremental journey which demands that I think and rethink my experience, moving constantly, often accompanied by a kind of psychic vertigo, from the present moment to the past and back into some further extended enlightenment. I did not begin with crass racial prejudices and move to the realization that "all people are alike," to a state of color blindness that many white people still believe to be the essence of a nonracist perspective. On the contrary, in a way, I was raised by white American radicals to believe in color blindness as an ideal and a reality and have come to understand that although it remains an ideal, we are very far indeed from its realization. We have racialized our society and our individual lives to such a degree that the problem of the color line, as W. E. B. Du Bois warned many years ago, is not only the central problem of the twentieth century, but will be of the twenty-first as well. Like any Black person I have ever known, I now perceive both obvious and subtle racism in the immediate world around me every single day.

My life has been dramatically altered by being the mother of Black sons over the course of more than twenty-five years. I record this story, I hope, in the best tone of a mother's voice, both reasoned and emotional, but always full of intensity. Whether in aesthetic forms or social life, it is the voice of privilege that wants ease, distance, linearity, perfect elegance, one convenient layer covering all the interwoven narratives of a life. Mine is not such a voice. Throughout the writing of this memoir I kept as my epigraph and talisman the concept of "imaginative identification" as used by the Nigerian writer Chinua Achebe. "Imaginative identification is the opposite of indifference," he tells us in an essay called "The Truth of Fiction." "It is human connectedness at its most intimate. . . . It begins as an adventure of self-discovery and ends in wisdom and humane conscience."

This is the story of a change in a white person's vision through self-discovery to conscience. It is the story of the education of an American woman.

"*Things are then not merely happening* before *us; they are happening, by the power and force of imaginative identification,* to *us. We do not only see; we* suffer *alongside the hero and are branded with the same mark.*" — *Chinua Achebe, "The Truth of Fiction*"

"*Is there not something unseemly in our society about the spectacle of a white woman mothering a black child? A white woman giving totally to a black child; a black child totally and demandingly dependent for everything, sustenance itself, from a white woman. The image of a white woman suckling a black child . . . Such a picture says, there is no difference; it places the hope of continuous generation, of immortality of the white self in a little black face.*"
— *Patricia J. Williams,* The Alchemy of Race and Rights

ONE.

THE RICHMOND

MUSEUM OF THE

CONFEDERACY

To liberate themselves from the curse of racism and the damage it inflicts upon white souls as well as black souls and black bodies, whites must in a sense "become black," must become involved in a process of liberation of the blacks . . . in the cities, in the towns, before the law, and in the mind. — James Baldwin *(from an interview in* Time, *May 17, 1963)*

[W]e talk about the way white people who shift locations . . . begin to see the world differently. Understanding how racism works, [they can see] the way in which whiteness acts to terrorize without seeing [themselves] as bad, or all white people as bad, and all black people as good. Repudiating us-and-them dichotomies does not mean we should never speak of the ways observing the world from the standpoint of "whiteness" may indeed distort perception, impede understanding of the way racism works both in the larger world as well as in the world of our intimate interactions. — *bell hooks,* Black Looks

In 1991 a special traveling exhibit was installed in the Richmond Museum of the Confederacy, a small collection of Civil War memorabilia and records in Richmond, Virginia. The exhibit, entitled "Before Freedom Came," contained photographs, artifacts, paintings, tapes of music and interviews, all pertaining to American slavery. I had come to see this exhibit along with more than a hundred other college teachers from universities across the country, all of us participating in a Ford Foundation grant to "explore multicultural perspectives in higher education," a nationwide effort to diversify college curricula.

I passed by the entrance to the permanent exhibitions on the first floor and headed up the wide staircase to the wing which, for the next several months, would house an addition to Virginia's traditional testimony to the Civil War.

Even after twenty years of living in a Black family, and at least ten years of teaching African American fiction and autobiography, I was not completely prepared for this face-to-face encounter with life-sized portraits of human beings who had been enslaved in the United States of America.

In an autobiographical essay about writing, Virginia Woolf talks about "moments of being"[1] — transforming and often suddenly conscious experiences when what she describes as the cotton wool of daily life is unexpectedly parted, and behind habits of ordinary consciousness one senses a truth, a *pattern,* as Woolf puts it, a perception of "what belongs to what." As I understand such moments, one does not experience a sudden conversion out of nowhere, proverbial veils falling from the eyes. Rather, changes long in the making coalesce. They slowly take shape in semi-conscious alterations of perspective, inchoate shifts one may be aware of only as vague discomfort, accumulations of small pieces of knowledge instantly "forgotten" or buried again, each time less fully, so that they surface with increasing frequency. And these changes of consciousness are often accompanied by the perception of a broader social context to one's own particular experience. Understanding where in the world your experience belongs enables you to know, or acknowledge, that it exists.

I had such an experience in the Richmond Museum that October day several years ago. More than twenty years before, in 1969, soon after I married Douglas and became a member of a Black American family, I became pregnant and, in the innocent, exultant power of the first day of a first and wanted pregnancy, I realized that I — my body and self — was no longer exactly white. Yet, I was still maintaining a determined color blindness common to whites and in those days certainly necessary for me. Race does not matter, will not matter for my child, I told myself, adhering by habit to the principle I had been raised with by the Jewish American radicals who were my family and early teachers.

But during the next twenty years I would undergo a transformation of consciousness as defining as any I have ever known. So, it was not that I came to understand the facts and implications of American slavery for the first time that day in the Richmond Museum. This would not have been possible for me, living in a Black family for so many years as I raised my sons from infancy to young manhood, all the while studying works by African American writers. Nevertheless, confronted with a sequence of rooms which recorded in stark, powerful visual images the story of American slavery, the *pattern* of my experience came into sharp and explicit focus. I saw my country, its history, and therefore myself differently, a difference that in key ways would change the way I saw everything and therefore the way I lived.

The first room contains large photographs of African Americans who worked as slave labor on southern plantations and farms. I stare into the faces of men, women, and children, their brows deeply knitted, dark eyes communicating grief and rage, a knowledge of human evil so unmitigated, all capacity for innocence seems instantly swept away. The only other place I've seen this expression is in photographs of concentration camp victims or, more recently, in television images of displaced refugees of starvation and war. Their eyes seem to warn me that I am about to see what they have seen, sights I cannot possibly anticipate in my imagination.

In a portrait off to the left, a young man is dressed in a suit and tie; he plays an accordian, an instrument usually associated with the pleasurable mood of parties and folk dancing. But his eyes are thick with sorrow, a deep misery which must be grotesquely contradicted by the lilting tones of his accordian. Had he grown up with no parent to care for him? Had he watched his wife beaten and raped, his children sold? Suddenly, I am seeing the ridges of scarred flesh from repeated whippings across his back, beneath the formal black jacket he wears. He is identified only as the slave of the southern general Robert E. Lee.

My mind is crowded with the voices of writing students over the course of many years talking about the crucial importance of personal voice, and of the connections between voice and naming one's own experience, naming the self; the importance of naming; of names. Here is the slave of Robert E. Lee, I believe I whispered out loud. And he has no name.

I am magnetized by his eyes. I feel something familiar and dark open inside me—a state of heightened awareness which always seems to involve the entwining of my own life with something outside of myself. I cannot *know* this "slave of Robert E. Lee" nor certainly claim his experience which is so different from my own. And yet in some way long known to me as a reader and writer of fiction, I am beginning to imagine his story, even to feel, perhaps, a sense of his suffering. I am aware of the dangers of presuming too much, yet I do not want to relinquish the burden of this connection, this "imaginative identification."[2] This phrase, used by the Nigerian writer Chinua Achebe, means, I believe, our capacity to understand and feel the suffering of another even though we have never experienced that particular suffering ourselves. Imaginative identification is intensified—it matures, so to speak—as one comes to know oneself more and more fully. For me, this has always been the task of autobiographical writing, the pursuit of an ever-stronger link between what Achebe calls "self-discovery and humane conscience."

Now I recall a recent evening when I was listening to a background of radio news as I cooked dinner. I heard a short special report on the life of Robert E. Lee, marking some historical occasion related to the Civil War. Hearing the valorizations and respectful descriptions of his character, I vaguely remembered elementary and high school lessons in American history in which the leader of the Confederate army was depicted as a great American and a great general, a depiction which always posited as secondary, even parenthetical at times, his relation to slavery. And I thought, we — white Americans — neither see the reality of slavery in our history, nor acknowledge the meaning of Black Americans living for centuries in "our" country. (My original family has been in this country for two generations. I am first generation American. Yet the phrase "our country" comes more easily to me, less packed down with potentially explosive contradictions, than it would to my husband and children.) If we focused on the fact that Lee owned slaves and fought for slavery, would we find ourselves in a historical mudslide, a confusion of collective identity too paradoxical to endure? Almost all of our founding fathers owned slaves, after all. What would making that reality a central one to the study of American history do to our sense of ourselves as a democracy? The stakes are high; we would have to engage in historical revision of the most pervasive kind, at the very least to recognize the stunning moral ambivalences we can apparently deny, the moral paradoxes we can abide. How might our children feel about great men who accomplished much for democracy and military history, *yet owned human beings,* if the emphasis of that sentence were turned around in their lessons. *He enslaved other people and fought for the system of slavery to continue, although he was also a great general.*

What do I, a Jewish woman, feel if Germany valorizes Nazi generals, no matter how brave and dedicated they may have been? I do not admire them as inspiring heroes who, on the side, devised elaborate plans and techniques for destroying human beings in numbers of torturous and efficient ways. Hearing such portraits of German military genius, or stories of fatherly devotion, I am disgusted, outraged: I know which is the more important truth. Listening to the profile on the news, for a moment I became my sons, Black Americans listening to the story of an American hero, Robert E. Lee.

As I make my way through the museum gallery, passing before the large photographs which cover nearly an entire wall, I hear my footsteps on the marble floor, the sound bringing back other, beloved museums: walls and walls of Van Goghs in the Metropolitan Museum in New York City, where I suddenly realized, as if never before knowing what I must have known, that a painting about death can also be a painting about yellow and blue. That moment of exhilaration serves now as a harsh contrast to the series of portraits of field and house slaves, adults and children standing in front of the slave quarters or sitting cross-legged in the grass, staring full-faced into the camera. These are the faces of my children's ancestors, the generation of my husband's great-grandparents. One "house slave," a fair-skinned woman, has straight, dark hair pulled back into a neat braid or bun. Her high-necked, tight-bodiced dress suggests the English fashions of the times, but her eyes convey the immobilized shock one sees in the eyes of a recent mourner who can not yet take in what she knows to be true. Intentionally, I do not check the dates or place but rather imagine she is Sophie, grandmother of Lois Meadows-White, my mother-in-law and friend.

By the time Lois was five, her own parents were dead, and she frequently stayed with her grandmother in a one-room shack in Trenton, North Carolina. From the newspapers which lined the walls for insulation during the often cold North Carolina winters, the grandmother practiced reading with the young child. "How come you can read, Granmammie?" Lois asked, old enough to understand that reading by one so old was completely unusual, a fact that merited amazement even to a six-year-old. The answer, which Lois has told me she would not comprehend for some years, was: "Because I lived in the house."

It seems relatively easy to distinguish the house slave in the photograph by her dress and carefully arranged hair. The "field slaves" are dressed in looser, shabbier clothes, the women's hair wrapped in turbans and scarves, or cut short, tiny curls shaped to the head in a style we might today call an Afro or a natural. The women "in the house" tend to have braided or rolled hair; straighter, pulled tightly away from neat parts, more like "white hair," and they have fairer skin, obviously the result of white paternity.

Richard Mentor Johnson of Kentucky, elected vice president in 1836, had two daughters, Adaline and Imogene, whom he failed to claim because their mother was a Black woman, a slave. In a political cartoon done at the time, someone presents the two girls to him at an official gathering.[3] He recognizes his children, but is horrified at the public unmasking. As he turns from them, holding his head in his hand, the two girls, dressed in the flowing gowns worn by the upper classes of the time, present him with a portrait of their mother.

South Carolina's "leading man of letters," William Gilmore Simms, in his *Morals of Slavery,* defended the accepted practice of rape of Black women as a "beneficial institution because it protected the purity of white women by allowing slaveholders to vent their lust harmlessly upon slave women."[4]

"Slavery is terrible for men; but it is far more terrible for women," wrote Harriet Jacobs in the classic slave narrative *Incidents in the Life of a Slave Girl.* "Superadded to the burden common to all, *they* have wrongs, and sufferings, and mortifications peculiarly their own."[5] She is speaking of rape and the selling away of children.

A young white boy leans comfortably against the shoulder of his "Louisiana Nursemaid," her eyes conveying that by-now-familiar grief which can easily be mistaken for emptiness. Was her own child sold away, perhaps, replaced by her "young charge"[6] because her child's features too closely resembled the master's? Or was her child's father a field slave whom she loved, child and husband separated from her because their color was dark brown, their place on a lower rung of the ladder of relative humanness?

How can I escape the weight of this so recent history when a Black woman who does not know me encounters me on the street, at a meeting, or party, obviously attached to a Black man? I feel neither guilt nor regret nor any sense of personal defensiveness for my choice of a husband. An obsessively self-conscious person, I am very clear about the deeply rooted origins which tied me for life to this person, and these roots are unquestionably more defining than racial or cultural differences. And of course, I know many Black women who are not bothered by white women coupled with Black men in particular cases, friends of mine, members of our family, who accept me fully as an individual. But there is also a social context and history to any personal decision or act.

I go to a party honoring a good friend who has recently been promoted to an important position. He is Black. His wife is white. I know these two people well and, as with my own marital history, I know they fell in love with each other as individuals. I even know them well enough to think I can begin to imagine the specifics of spirit and personal history that drew them to one another. I do not doubt the complete authenticity, the humanity beyond race, of their attachment as I never doubted that same authenticity in my nearly thirty-year attachment to Douglas. Yet, as I wind my way through the crowded party, held in a splendid apartment on the upper west side of Manhattan, full of progressive leaders in government, social agencies, the arts, I see numerous "interracial" couples, all Black men and white women. There are Black women there too, of course, and they seem to be with Black men or on their own. My personal experience, however unique, is also part of a historical process, a broader narrative framing my individual story, not completely defining it nor even, perhaps, substantially changing it, but touching it, affecting it. We do not exist outside of history, our lives uncomplicated by what came before.

I return my attention to the center of the large gallery, where I turn slowly as the portraits begin to ebb and flow like some rhythmic sea, swaying toward me, then back against the walls, and I feel engulfed by faces which seem alive for a moment, reflections of spirits no longer confined to two-dimensional space. I walk past large paintings, then black and white photographs of people occasionally named: Omar ibn Said, a Muslim brought to South Carolina as a young man; he fled, was apprehended and attracted attention by writing in Arabic on his prison walls.[7] More often the identification is simply: "unknown Africans," and for a moment's relief from these faces whose names and histories have been lost, I begin to look around at the other visitors standing beside me.

Except for our mixed group of teachers and professors, nearly everyone is Black. Like me, many carry small journals in which they jot down quick notes, shaking their heads in disbelief or despair at this record of human depravity and degradation. Overheard conversations invoke contemporary works of fiction, especially *Beloved* by Toni Morrison, that great novel about the dark heart of American history. "Even Frederick Douglass' narrative of his life in slavery and his escape does not prepare you for the visual shock," I hear someone say. Many other people write nothing, simply look, people who seem to be from various walks of life — teachers, I imagine, or nurses, civil service workers, housecleaners, parents. Young people on an assignment from school gather in small groups as all of us participate in this double witnessing: we, the late-twentieth-century witnesses to the faces of the original witnesses. We do not see what they see, but in their eyes we see the evidence of what they see.

A heavy-set, muscular Black man wearing a plaid shirt and jeans, several books tucked under his arm, his hands folded tightly across his stomach, stares for a long moment at one group portrait and asks, "Incredible, isn't it?" I answer, yes, feeling deeply relieved by this tiny moment of connection. Tears fill my eyes, until the faces around me, visitors and photographs, blur slightly, as though a fine rain has suddenly begun to fall, and I am terribly, visibly, shamefully white. It is a familiar feeling, one I often experience in the company of Black people when questions involving race and racism arise. How to speak? Anything said by a white person, still living the legacy of it all so intensely, seems gratuitous and presumptuous.

As writing these words here can suddenly seem gratuitous — *there are so many books by Africans and African Americans, more than a century of fiction, autobiographical narrative, theory.* And this telling of my experience can seem presumptuous — *What can I know, can I possibly have to say?*

Doubt of white authenticity among Blacks might as well be built into the cells by now. It starts early in childhood when the searing disappointments begin to occur. I recall the first time Adam, when he was three years old, was called "nigger" — his running home to tell us about the child who had called him a "bad word"; the first time Khary, when he was eleven or twelve, was followed in a store. I was in another aisle shopping for some small thing when he came toward me, looking over his shoulder nervously as the shop owner kept a close watch on his every move. Humor and perspective remain, of course, even at times some comfort with well-known whites who have proven their understanding, their need to know. My sons feel most comfortable with white members of their extended family who take an open interest in race and acknowledge the reality, as well as their own ignorance, of the stress of every single day for Black people in this country. Then I will sense an ability and willingness in them to relinquish the posture of self-defense, a relaxation into ordinary humanness. "I understand you" is often less authentic, and therefore less comforting, than "What are you going through?" On the other hand, "Oh, who would bother you on the street," some well-intentioned white friend will say. "A big, strapping (Black) guy like you." Stated or unstated, the adjective in parentheses is there. At such times a wall is hit, and it is no longer possible to be ordinary. Innocence and vulnerability are destroyed or masked by anger and suspicion. A good, workable defense. It grows with the years. It takes root. I have witnessed this process in my children.

"I am so happy to be in a place where I can be friends mostly with Black kids," Khary says to me on the phone after his first weeks at college. "We have so much in common."

I am happy for his comfort, for his having found a kind of home away from home at school. But then I wonder, as I have done many times since my sons reached adolescence and began their lives as *young Black men in America:* Do my children think of me as white before or after they think "my mother"? How soon after? Does it seem *personal* to them, a neutral fact of their identities — a Jewish mother, as someone might have a Jamaican father — or does it touch off even a flashing moment of regret, an unbridgeable distance between us?

This recent sense of visibility I experience in my own family is not a result of my sons' unusual or extreme beliefs. Neither of them is "separatist" or prejudiced. It is a consequence of their seeing the world as they must, as Black people. It is significant, of course, that I am a first-generation Jewish woman whose father was raised in the Jewish ghetto of Kishenev. These facts are part of my heritage, they have contributed to my story, and thus to the family stories my children carry within themselves. But no particular heritage can erase the story of my whiteness, the fact, for instance, that I am welcome, seen as perfectly ordinary, in certain places where my children would not be welcome, never seen as ordinary.

Most of the time whites and Blacks live entirely separate lives. I went to a matinee in New York City recently, a delightful musical, accompanied by a good friend. I saw immediately that there was not one single brown face in the audience or in the play. My older son, Adam, is an actor now, and I thought: he could not even audition for these parts, nor for parts in many other productions, although race is not an issue in the plot in any way. Agents send Black actors for auditions only when race is specified, he tells me. When there is no specification, only white clients are sent. After the play, my friend and I went for a drink at a nearby hotel. Again, I traveled in a white world, comfortably invisible in a way I would never be if I were with my family. Even in this multiracial city, in apartment buildings, schools, restaurants, entertainment centers of all kinds, there is a corridor of unalleviated whiteness. No longer a segregation legally enforced, it is there all the same. Most of the time, there are two different worlds, and I see it, feel it, am no longer privileged to be blind to it, as most white people are.

In the next large room of the museum, I am looking at a plain rag doll made of what looks like unbleached muslin, a tie near the top to fashion a head, two knots of thread for eyes, a line of thread for a mouth. The doll was left behind by an unidentified child on a plantation in Durham, North Carolina. Where was the mother of the child who left the doll behind? Had she been sold away? The catalog which I read off and on as I move through the silent awesome rooms says: "An Arkansas slave was brought to the auction block without knowing her master intended to sell her . . . They had to get some men to throw her down and hold her to keep her from going back to the house. They sold her away from her baby boy."[8]

Children were forcibly taken from their mothers frequently, of course.

I write this sentence not because I think it represents some new knowledge, but because I know we must repeat it and repeat it in order to bring it to the surface of American consciousness. It tends to drown in a sea of repression, denial, and callousness; it tends to sink down. *They sold her away from her baby boy.* I try to feel this mother, ripped away from her child, as I read the unadorned language, a simple declarative sentence: Children were taken from their mothers with frequency.

The tension between separation and connection is perhaps the most fundamental, psychic theme of motherhood. From the dramatic, painful hours of birth-giving, to the nearly inconceivable horror of outliving one's children, mothers are challenged to make sense of this me/not me feeling we have about our children. None of the psychological platitudes about "letting them go" and "holding them close" come near to describing the actual loss or the passion. In war and other enormous upheavals, these are the most poignant images: A dead Somalian baby, skeletal and fly-infested, being torn from its mother's arms for burial. A Bosnian soldier's mother sitting by her dying son's side, staring at him intensely as if her uncompromising vigilance might bring him back to life. In American slavery, this tearing apart was institutionalized over the course of more than 200 years, over fourteen generations. With institutionalization comes a kind of obliviousness among those not being directly hurt.

In only ten years or so we have become increasingly inured to the homeless among us. I walk past many individuals who, five years ago, I'd have been unable to walk past, and so I am diminished in my humanness. What sort of diminishment took place in white Americans who witnessed this tearing apart of mothers and children and in white Americans who remain oblivious to this piece of our history today?

In one photograph, a father holds a small child on one hip, his other hand grasping a hoe or rake. And I think about how children were taken, with equal frequency, from their fathers. There is no way I can refrain, nor should perhaps, from imagining my own children taken from their father, Douglas, whose graceful hands I now remember diapering them, rocking them, tossing them a ball, feeding them. I see him now, these two young men his closest friends in the world. Douglas is just fifty. He attended a Black college in Durham, North Carolina, where the rag doll was found. He grew up in a completely segregated world and only began to know white people well in his early twenties.

My children have heard stories of segregation throughout their childhood, grim stories and humorous stories, shared at our family dinner table. How their father, a state champion swimmer as a child, had to wait until he was nine to learn to swim because until then there was no "colored pool" in the town, and then he was forbidden to compete against white teams. How their grandmother sent her children to Catholic schools which, although equally segregated, were nevertheless superior to the segregated public schools. "We had some old movie house," their father, the movie lover, will say, "where we had the second-run movies after they finished playing in the white theaters." How the sit-ins at local lunch counters and Holiday Inns, the demonstrations against all white movie theaters and downtown stores were the defining experiences of reclaimed autonomy and a sense of dignity for their father when he was about the age they are now. How he and their grandmother, uncles, and aunt went to American jails for this illegal activity. The United States of America: 1950s and 1960s. No remote legacy, these are the years of my own childhood, just as Lois's childhood memories include the story of her grandmother, a former slave, helping her read from newspapers on the wall of a shack in Trenton, North Carolina.

Yet in years of teaching African American literature I have learned that the overwhelming majority of white American students are shocked to realize the recentness of this history. They have been raised and educated to think that slavery happened very long ago, just as they have been taught to believe that racism has long since ceased to exist in most parts of this country. As one student put it: Slavery was always back then, and racism was always out there.

One of my clearest and most treasured childhood memories is of my father, who raised my sister and me alone after our mother's early death, telling stories of life in the *shtetle,* the grim memories of the *pogroms*—how he and his family hid, and finally emerged when the violence was spent, and how they survived. Listening to him tell the story of his

childhood, of his long trek across Europe, his emigration to America —
stories told as he speared a piece of hard rye bread with a long knife and
offered it around the table — I understood that life in the Jewish ghettos
of Eastern Europe and Russia could never be just academic history to
me. My father's life as a poor Russian Jew, then as an American immigrant, is lodged in the deepest layers of my psyche — the way I move, the
way I speak at times, even the way I feel. His reverse English syntax will
suddenly penetrate my own educated grammatical structures: *This is a
way to behave?* I would hear myself ask my children when they were
disobedient. Although I do not speak Yiddish and retain only a few key
phrases of endearment and irony from that rich and vibrant language, I
would sometimes cry, *My precious shane ingeleh* — beautiful little boy —
when my passion for them rose into speech.

In the same way, Douglas's stories are embedded in the psyches of
Adam and Khary, two young Black men of the 1990s, the *first* legally
integrated generation in the United States of America.

Yet we are told from many quarters that "race" does not matter, should
not matter, and so should not be spoken as a reference to something
which cannot refer to anything at all. We are informed that our country has transcended racism and even color consciousness, that certain
Black heroes, from athletes to politicians, have "transcended race" which
means only that these individuals are somehow acceptable to white
America. Dutifully, we surround the word *race* with quotation marks
because we know that as a biological category, race does not really exist.
It is as if, looking at what we have made of race, like our own home-
grown Medusa snakes flying from her head, will turn us to stone.

Petrified: turned to stone. I focus on that word as I walk through the
museum where, now, I hear music — work songs, spirituals, blues, the
Black American music that records so much unrecorded history and
teaches the lessons still untaught in most American schools. The music
increases the emotional intensity of witnessing. Next to the rag doll is a
whip, then wrist shackles, and more ordinary "artifacts" — a pottery bowl
used for grinding corn, a beautifully carved wooden pew, "probably
made by a slave." Petrified. The word has come to mean terrified, so

deeply frightened one is immobilized, paralyzed — as if turned to stone. Perhaps as Americans we have been traumatized by this grotesque and horrifying secret in our past, a secret which, like many family secrets, is really known by us all and is now more often being spoken aloud in many places, it is true, but which is still, in most classrooms, in many circles, treated as ugly or frightening family secrets are often treated: with ruthless denial. I mean this secret of slavery and how it sits at the heart of our history and manifests itself in so much of our present. I don't mean that we deny its historical reality, but that as in many secrets of family pathology, we deny its central importance. How might this truth, if faced, change everything about the way we write and teach and think and feel about ourselves? What might happen if white Americans looked squarely at our own American history? For as soon as we name ourselves Americans, we must claim this history for better or for worse, no matter how recently arrived our families. "I am an American," my father used to say proudly in his heavily accented English, Russian pronunciations and Yiddish rhythms composing the odd harmonies of his speech. *An American.* By which I know he meant that he claimed for his life's core the values of democracy, equality of opportunity, and cultural freedom. His name is inscribed on the wall at Ellis Island. But there are no names inscribed in that wall of Adam and Khary's ancestors from the other side of their family, immigrants of another sort. No inscriptions on that wall. No names remembered.

And no permanent slavery museum in this country, though now, following the model of Yad Vashem in Jerusalem, a Holocaust museum exists in Washington, D.C.

Some years ago, I traveled to Jerusalem with Douglas, and the first place we visited was Yad Vashem, the Holocaust Museum. Before entering the rooms of that almost religious site, our group was repeatedly told by the guide: Here is the museum of the Holocaust. You cannot understand anything about Israel without understanding this.

In one of the halls of that museum a list of concentration camps was engraved into the walls. Beneath the names of the camps, among other exhibits, was a collection of drawings done by children while living in the camps, and these alternated with photographs of children who stared at us through lines of barbed wire, like the faces of American slaves look at me now. An old man dressed in black sat on a bottom stair, his arms flung across his knees, gazing ahead at the imagery of fire, stick trees, guns, birds, and the sun, and silently he wept.

As I stare at the white rag doll and remember the children's drawings, thinking about the complex ways some secrets are revealed, others maintained, and of the ancient Jewish recognition of the need for remembering, I suddenly realize I am standing in an American Yad Vashem, a museum of a holocaust inadequately remembered and insufficiently grieved. And just as I begin to hear a humming and shouting, sounds I remember from the halls of the Museum of the Holocaust in Jerusalem, I am confronted by a large, glass display case, its horrifying "artifact" rising seven feet into the air.

Here is the infamous harness. An iron belt is joined to an iron leash which leads up to an iron necklace from which the leash leads upward again to a bell, which hangs several feet over a man's head so that, like a cow apt to graze beyond allocated land into forbidden pastures, his movements can be followed. In this way, the slave master can hear the bell ring and know the *thing* he owns, the animal (the person redefined as animal/thing so that any violence is possible) is following his own intention and may therefore be becoming dangerous.

I am standing before this iron icon, and at the same moment it is seven years before and I am gazing into a large case holding dozens of yellow Stars of David at Yad Vashem. I notice the tiny white, blue, black threads still visible along the sides of the star where the yellow cloth of indisputable identification: *Jude,* was sewn to the darker fabric of a jacket, a sweater, a coat. Then I am standing in a wing of the new Ellis Island Museum, a room that records not the welcoming shores of an America dedicated to liberty and inclusion, but instead presents the other nation we all know exists, a nation, like most other places, filled with people who hate. Arranged in a long, horizontal pattern on the wall are warning signs and journals, articles, and advertisements, forbidding Irish to apply, denouncing wops and kikes and spicks and niggers, cartoons depicting "big-lipped niggers" and "long-nosed Jews." Advertisements for jobs and places to live seek "white Christians," language both coded and brazen telling one of the stories of our lives.

Now I mark the rusted edges of the metal leash, the ordinary familiarity and grotesque humiliation of the bell, then see, to my left, a large poster advertising the "Sale of Valuable Slaves." As with the now-famous photographs of concentration camp victims piled on top of each other in naked, nearly undifferentiated masses of human bone, no one who has not seen an actual advertisement for the sale of human beings can imagine its paralyzing horror. Moral abstractions fade in the explosive impact of *Sarah, aged 45; Dennis, her son, a mulatto, age 24* (who is "smart and of first rate character"); *Fanny, age 16; Mary Ann, age 7, a Creole who speaks French; Emma, an orphan, aged 10 or 11.* Next to this another plaque quoting Louisa Picquet, a child who, as she was being taken away by her new owner, heard, "someone cryin' and prayin' the Lord to go with her only daughter, and protect me . . . Mother was right on her knees," Louisa tells us, "with her hands up, prayin' to the lord for me. She didn't care who saw her: The people all lookin' at her. I often thought her prayers followed me, for I could never forget her."[9]

My vision clears. Hearing returns. A tape is being played somewhere, as if the voice is coming from the walls or the floor beneath my feet. Paul Robeson's unmistakable baritone singing, "No more auction block for me, many thousands gone."

I am not a Holocaust survivor, neither the descendant of American slaves nor of slave holders, not myself an immigrant to American shores. But I am the distant cousin of Holocaust victims, the child of an immigrant Jew, the daughter-in-law of a woman who remembers her grandmother telling stories of her childhood in slavery, the mother of two young Black men who are the fifth free-born generation of people enslaved for fourteen generations.

All this is my history and I come from all of this. When I walk through the white world, I am a white woman who generally blends in, who is not looked at with suspicion or fear or even hatred when I walk down a beautiful ocean beach in New England or northern California where my children's brown bodies instantly stand out differently than does mine, their skins beautiful and rich brown against the water and sand. I am an ordinary American woman protected by this whiteness (which, we all know, does not really exist yet is known and visible and powerful) into a precious invisibility of apparent belonging, and I am weighted down with the transforming shame this knowledge brings.

As I look back at the iron harness, my knees literally bending so I have to concentrate hard in order to remain standing, I see an old man has walked up next to me. He is dressed in a worn, black suit, shiny with age. His white collar, slightly frayed but carefully pressed by some attentive hand, is buttoned up right to the neck. His trimmed beard is nearly all white but the tight curls which push out from his grey, felt hat are still partly black, not fully taken over by the grey. His skin is dark brown so that its aged creases around the mouth, the eyes, across the forehead, look dark purple or black. He leans heavily on an old wooden cane, the kind you can buy in drugstores. And he weeps. Like the old man at Yad Vashem before the children's drawings, he silently weeps. No sobbing, just plentiful tears falling from his lids down his cheeks, the slightly glowing rivulets disappearing inside his pressed white collar. And beyond embarrassment, I stop fighting my knees, I let them buckle and, crouching on the floor, I weep too.

It is clear to me that day that although I have much to read, learn, plan, and experience, I will find some way as a white teacher to teach the slave narratives to my white students, to help them not turn to stone. And I will somehow find the words to teach this narrative history to Black students among whom I shall have to tread with utmost care, proving and reproving what I do understand, acknowledging as respectfully as I can what I do not.

In the next room, I hear a taped interview conducted by a WPA worker in the 1930s. An old man who had been a slave told of his white mother, a young daughter of a slave-holding family in North Carolina, who was confined to an attic prison on the day her small child, fathered by a Black man, was sold away. "I believe they told her I was being sold just down

the road to where my father's mama was a slave," he says almost mus-
ingly. "But in reality I was being sold down to Texas. Naturally, I never
saw her again." His mother's name was Jane, the same as my own.

Whether coincidence or some more mystical and mysterious coordina-
tion of the details of life, this small identification seems the perfect symbol for the intricate confluence of learning, memory, and feeling of the
past few hours. I am thinking about that other Jane as I descend the wide
staircase into the permanent exhibits of the museum where I move from
large, colorful paintings of military heroes on white horses, to the preserved cannon that defended the city of Richmond, to the uniform,
complete with medals for valor and bravery, of some leading officer in
the Confederate Army. In the paintings all the foreground faces are
white. When Blacks appear, they are smiling gratefully, pathetic victims,
their outlines fading into earth and sky.

I look up the stairway at the travelling exhibit, "Before Freedom
Came," and I am horrified by the realization that in two months the
slavery exhibits will have gone on to another city, leaving the historical
deception and moral lie of the Museum of the Confederacy on its own
again.

*Supposing this had been the case at Yad Vashem, and upon leaving that
museum I descended to a floor that celebrated the military successes of Nazi
Germany — as if the two testimonials could exist, calmly and unconflictually,
side by side?*

Now, the Richmond Museum becomes a metaphor for American denial of the reality of slavery and of African American history as a central core of American history, standing for all the collisions of our best
hopes and worst cruelties, collisions still erupting (unsurprisingly —
ungrieved, not fully known) in dramatic violence today. I recall the hum
I seemed to hear during the most intense moments at Yad Vashem, again
as I walked through the slavery exhibits. Now the hum becomes a drum
beat — the drum which was prohibited by southern slave masters who
understood its powerful communicative purposes, its reminder of history and message of resistance. The drum beats and my vision changes.

African American history and culture is not a subject to add to American education. There is no American education without it.

Since that day in the Richmond Museum, I have been motivated by this awakening, through reading, teaching and, now, writing, to make some small contribution to re/membering (putting back together the dis/membered parts) of this monumental, ongoing American story of race hatred and racialized life. I write not only as a white mother of Black sons, but as a Jewish woman — not observant, secular — but the daughter of immigrants, steeped all of my life in what I can only call Jewish sensibility and culture — and I am angered by the contrasts between these two cultural rememberings — the morally active remembering of one genocide; the half-blind refusal to adequately remember the other. This terrible contrast has of course played itself out in my sons' experience with even more painful rending than it has in my own. Black and Jewish, raised in a nonreligious home, coming of age as young Black men at a time when their very lives are in danger from several directions simply because they are young Black men, they had learned, by the time they were ten or twelve, that most white Jews saw them as "different" — at best not quite Jewish or not Jewish at all, but always as Black. By the time they were in their teens, they had come to know themselves as Black men, an identification that seemed not only right to me but sane. Meanwhile, negotiating the complex maternal roads that paralleled their growth into manhood, overstepping boundaries between self and others as mothers so often do, becoming most at home in the borderlands between conventionally distinguished identities, I would come to see myself as an "interracial" person in a family of Black Americans.

From that perspective it is clear to me that as with the memory of the Holocaust in Israel, without understanding slavery, we cannot understand the United States of America. And from that perspective it was clear to me that I would have to revisit the story of my life in a Black family if I wanted to center a focus that is too easily marginalized for any white person thus distorting and even erasing the truth.

TWO.

COLOR BLIND:

THE WHITENESS

OF WHITENESS

And there was something so foul in that, something in the crime of innocence so revolting it paralyzed him. He had not known because he had not taken the trouble to know. He was satisfied with what he did know. Knowing more was inconvenient and frightening. Like a bucket of water with no bottom. If you know how to tread, bottomlessness need not concern you. — Toni Morrison, Tar Baby

In the Prologue of Ralph Ellison's *Invisible Man,* a preacher speaks to his congregation: "Brothers and Sisters, my text this morning is the 'Blackness of Blackness.'"

Some years ago, Gary Lemons, a colleague of mine, gave that term — The Blackness of Blackness — to the title of a course in which he explored with students the often hidden cultural, personal, moral meanings of Blackness in literature by African Americans.[1]

Intrigued and educated by his conceptualization, I began searching for an understanding of the Blackness of Blackness, even if from the perspective of an outsider/stranger. I have kept a mental record that moves among different layers of consciousness. I read and study literature, its themes and practice, some history, and I listen to a lot of music. Intense focus tends to break down resistances to new consciousness, and I try to attend as carefully as possible to the details of my family's experiences. Years ago, I dreamed repeatedly of wandering in Africa, a blinding sun keeping me away from home. And so I remained for years in a sparse but beautiful room where I had to return again and again, each time I missed my plane back to New York City. For some time, as I became increasingly involved with my children's African heritage, I interpreted this dream as a turn on the word son, for sun: a representation of the dangerous loss of self and creative transcendance of self that is the ambivalent heart of motherhood. Looking back on that state of creative wandering that is the first stage of any deep change in me, I came to understand that any appreciation of the Blackness of Blackness would have to be accompanied by a willingness to explore whiteness. It was love that kept me from this realization so long. I did not want to be different from Douglas and especially my children. Being Jewish was something we might share, but whiteness was the sign of their greatest troubles and I was afraid of getting lost without them. When I thought back on my recurring dream, I saw that the blindness was always in the form of a white light.

Not for a moment do I diminish the difficulty of the task. As I begin to write about whiteness, remembering blindness as well as seeing, afraid of offending, of sentimental guilt, of being just plain wrong, I call up for myself the words I use to en/courage — give courage to — students embarking on the project of autobiographical writing, a project whose dangers they always underestimate:

> "And of course I am afraid, because the transformation of silence into language and action is an act of self-revelation, and that always seems fraught with danger." Audre Lorde, *Sister/Outsider*[2]

"[W]e cannot wait for the undamaged to make our connections for us; we can't wait to speak until we are perfectly clear and righteous. There is no purity and, in our lifetimes, no end to this process." Adrienne Rich, "Split At The Root."[3]

But where can I find the stories, silenced and distorted by years of denial and blindness, as the most important stories often are — my students have asked me.

Start with recent memories and work backward, I tell them. Memory leads to consciousness, recollection to the possibility of meaning which always includes a perception of relation between oneself and the world. This is the central principle of an autobiographical attitude we shall try to practice and name.

It is 1992, and Khary is eighteen, a freshman in college. Although he attends a largely white institution, there are enough Black students (98 in the freshmen class) for him to choose a Black social world. Because he concentrates in African and African American Studies, he is often spared the difficulties of being the only Black person in an all-white class, a condition he experienced throughout his high school years in the progressive private school we sent him to, where covert, pervasive racism nevertheless penetrated and often ruined his days. He is clearly happier than he has been in years. He loves his friends, Black Americans, Caribbean, and African students, several of them with one white parent like himself, who nevertheless define themselves, as he does, as Black.

I am slowly introduced to their perspective on identity. Black Americans have been so-called mixed since the days of slavery, and many still are. Frederick Douglass, who escaped to freedom on September 3, the day of Khary's birth, had a white father, as did many other slaves. Like Douglass, my son tells me, he does not qualify his Blackness. Political and personal life are neatly separated only in academic abstractions. As a feminist, a teacher of feminist studies, as a woman, I know this: the straight, unblurred line between collective and personal stories is an illusion of privilege.

"The world gets inside your head," one Latina student said last semester, defending Jane Eyre's internalized self-doubt, her sometimes overly righteous conviction, to a classmate who criticized that early feminist heroine for her lapses and weaknesses in the face of dominating, erotic love.

"I am Black," Khary explains to me repeatedly during that first year away from home when he has to find and take his place in his own world. "I have a Jewish mother, but I am not 'biracial.' That term is meaningless to me. I reject the identity of the tragic mulatto." He goes on to explain his beliefs and feelings in detail, and when I say, "I understand," he tells me carefully, gently, "I don't think you do, Mom. You can't understand this completely because you're white."

At first, I am slightly stunned, by his vehemence and by the idea. Perhaps even more than most mothers, I have identified with my children. Like other writers of my generation, I have used the experience of motherhood to try to comprehend the essential human conflict between devotion to others and obligations to the self, the lifelong tension between the need for clear boundaries and boundless intimacy. A motherless daughter since early childhood, I have experienced difficulty but also real reparation in mothering children myself. Now, standing in a darkened hallway facing my son, I feel exiled from my not-yet-grown child.

Fierce possessiveness lies at the heart of motherhood right alongside the more reasonable need to see one's children become themselves, and now this emotion rises up and chokes me, obliterating vocabulary. I can not find words to express my feelings, or my feelings are too threatening to find easy language. They are mine fields lining opposite sides of the road of my motherhood of this beloved son. What is this whiteness that threatens to separate me from my own child? Why haven't I seen it lurking, hunkering down, encircling me in some irresistible fog? I want to say the thing that will be most helpful to him, offer some carefully designed, unspontaneous permission for him to discover his own road, even if that means leaving me behind. On the other hand, I want to cry out, don't leave me, as he cried to me when I walked out of day-care centers, away from baby-sitters, out of his first classroom in public school. And always, this double truth, as unresolvable as in any other passion, the paradox: she is me/not me; he is mine/not mine.

A close friend, a Black man who grew up in North Carolina with Douglas, has taken a special interest in Khary, and tells him one day: Your mother isn't really white. She's a Black person in disguise.

Warmed by the love and friendship I know the remark signifies and tempted to relax into its welcome, I also know its message is false. I am white, and I remember long years of childhood and early womanhood when I was as blind to the realities of race as any white American.

I was raised by American Communists who, apart from any of the controversial politics of that period or this one, instilled in their children values of human commonality and internationalist identification. Some of their methods and beliefs can seem ludicrously misguided (one of their favorite words for self-criticism) to the contemporary eye. There was a time, for instance, when the Communist Party was trying to eradicate racism from its ranks, when you could be brought up on charges (before a party tribunal) for ordering a "black and white" soda. "We are all the same, there are no differences between people," was the weird non sequitur in response to any childish notification of color differences among strangers or friends.

We were taught to sing, "You can get good milk from a brown-skinned cow, the color of the skin doesn't matter anyhow." But attributing brown skin to a Negro was considered insulting, a revelation of racial prejudice in itself. The obsessive denial that race mattered was obviously a white creation. I recall very vaguely one or two times when a Black comrade corrected our earnest white parents, suggesting that noticing Blackness was not by definition an offense. Perhaps someone may have tried to explain that invisibility from false tolerance could be just as insulting as invisibility from outright contempt. "Of course she sees I'm Black," I recall a tall, heavy-set man saying to my father who had criticized me for identifying the man's color — which I did, in part, because I was obsessed with color differences in everything, drawing and painting as a means of relief from a lonely and troubled childhood. In part, these memories are vague because, as time passed, I came to accept the idea that any color noticing was a failure of virtue, a departure from good values and an unmasking of prejudice. The moral commandment obliterated real memory, drove the shape of actual experience into a polluted mist of unidentifiable shame.

The memories are also vague, I think, because the experiences were so rare. Black people hardly ever entered the interiors of the intimate collective life of the Communist families I knew. Nearly as much as any other white American community, our life was white. The Blacks we saw most often, apart from the occasional famous artist/comrade who graced a party or meeting with his or her presence, were the women who worked for some of the families as housekeepers and caregivers.

My parents hired a series of women to substitute for my mother, who was a "career woman," a feminist in the terms of her day who worked under her "maiden" name and supported her family, allowing my father to continue his largely unpaid work as a party official. When I was seven and my sister four years old, our mother died after a long illness, and although our substantially lowered income brought us from a life of upper-middle-class privilege into the always money-conscious limitations of my father's working-class life, we nevertheless continued to be dependent on a paid housekeeper rather than the relatives a poorer family might have found to fill the gap.

Before my mother's illness, when my sister was just born, a young woman named Lavinia worked for us. She was harsh and punitive, and I recall very clearly her verbal threats — to lock me in the closet or throw me out the window — and several times being actually pushed or slapped. She was fired when I recounted these stories to my parents, and for many years I remembered the experience only as a source of anger at my parents' casual methods of choosing caretakers for us. When I was a young mother, sitting in the park with babies and toddlers day after day, and noticed the harshness of some Black women toward their young, white charges — which white mothers always notice and comment on righteously, congratulating themselves on staying home with their children — I remembered Lavinia and wondered about her life. I tried to imagine the racial animosities, class and cultural differences regarding standards of children's behavior which might have motivated her threats and slaps. I try to picture her now, but I have lost the memory of her features. I do recall telling her once that she was pretty; I see her hair pulled back behind her ears into a dark net, a slender body always in a white and grey uniform, a long brown arm reaching out to strike me when I tried to poke and scratch my baby sister through the bars of her crib.

After Lavinia, Rose came to work for us. She nursed my mother through her last months of life and, in effect, raised my sister and me for the next ten years. My father called her *Razela,* a Jewish endearment of her name, and like all the other Communists, insisted she was a "member of the family." Politely, softly, she would correct him. "I love you girls, and I love your father, but I work for him."

We ate her cooking, watched her iron our clothes, marveled at the hot comb she used to straighten her hair late at night when she occasionally slept at our house. We got to know her family and visited her small, neat Harlem apartment where the food smelled and tasted exotically different from the food she made for us. But we did not understand, nor were we taught, the simplest facts of her history or heritage. That she had been born in Georgia was all we knew, and had a son in his early twenties who was in the army, stationed in Germany. She had a "boyfriend" — a short, husky musician named Russel who visited our house and was extremely friendly to us. She took care of an aging mother who died while we were still children, but I have no memory of the nature, duration, or quality of Rose's grief.

I know that I did not really know her, and I know that I loved her in a typically childish way: I needed her. Her attentions and protection were essential to me. Her attitudes toward disciplinary clarity, even when harsh — attitudes I know now to be typically southern Black — were a welcome contrast to the immigrant Jewish ambivalence and ambiguity in all things that otherwise characterized our upbringing. If she said something, she meant it, for good or ill. This was new and comforting to me, and years later I would instantly recognize and be drawn to the same quality in Douglas.

She sang us "Summertime" and "Stormy Weather" and, when I had children, I sang those songs to them, hearing her slightly off-key melodies in my head.

Like the sound of my father's voice whispering Yiddish endearments — *ketsaleh, madeleh* — her language remains in my mind as signals of warmth and love — the phrase *Lord have mercy;* the word *ain't;* even *I'm gonna beat your behind.* The first time Douglas called me *Sugar* the echo that rang in me was the sound of her voice.

The hypocricies twisted into our attitudes toward race were the result of arrogance. Like their largely man-made views on "the woman question" which can now seem so hopelessly naive (it was important for mothers and eventually daughters to "work for a living" but there was no concept of shared housework or child care being an aspect of "women's liberation"; girls were expected to be "smart," but were ruthlessly judged on their looks and physical graces); similarly, their views on race were formed by whites who never, it seems, asked Blacks for their analyses or points of view.

Still, we were explicitly, even rigidly taught an ideology of fairness against the pervasive American tolerance of inequality and white supremacy, and therefore I have no doubt that even in the most racially divided and racist society, children can be taught not to hate. Sheer bigotry was never accorded the respectability of objective truth or even valid argument. I was made ready to learn. When I married Douglas, my father was surprised and pleased and soon, after getting to know him, began to brag incessantly about the strong and reliable "Negro chap" his often "crazy" daughter had married.

Shortly before his death (when Adam was barely two years old) my father began having a recurring dream. He was traveling across country with his beloved grandson who in the dream was nineteen or twenty, and they would be unable to find a room in a motel. My father would know that it was because of his grandson's race, and in a variety of ways in a number of different dreams he would begin to battle the racists and haters on his grandson's behalf. Always spiritually charged by the challenges of battle — a fighter by nature or by virtue of his difficult life as a Russian Jew, then as an American Communist — he fashioned his fantasies of victorious conflict from what he understood would be the most predictable burden of his grandson's life. He believed standing up for racial justice in his grandson's behalf would be sufficient, never imagining the hidden narratives of superiority and domination Blacks would identify in white behavior over the next twenty years. He lived in a more naive time for white Americans. I like to think he would have helped my children, coming of age in this difficult, racially polarized time, to hang on to a faith in a nonracial society, a dream to help shape reality, even as reality must demystify our dreams.

I face my younger son in the hallway on the first vacation of his first year away from home, and I watch his face, its bone structure sharpening into beautiful planes as he matures. For years he has towered over me and looks down on me now, his eyes filled with contradictory emotions of his own. He must assert himself, stand by who he is, yet without hurting me.

In the moment we stand there, searching for some new words in which to speak, in a long moment of silence that turns into a silent embrace, I feel my whiteness as a sun-blinded desert of distance from my sons.

When I decided to marry Douglas I had no thoughts of children or their problems, and if I considered their racial identity at all it was with a combination of denial of its importance and a naive faith in imminent, radical social change. It was the sixties and I was twenty-two years old. I had found a man who possessed a temperament which provided a kind of security and reliability utterly lacking in my own childhood, values I shared, and an understated but intense sensuality I desired. The fact that he was Black and I Jewish seemed irrelevant at a time when race relations were at the center of a radical revision of America. It was the time of the civil rights and Black Power movements in which we both had been and continued to be active in different ways.

We met on a picket line, the 1966 strike of public assistance workers against the New York City Welfare Department. It was a multiracial, multiethnic strike, and like the public school teachers whose labor movement battles I had been raised to support, we believed we walked the snowy streets that winter, carrying watery hot chocolate and printed placards, for the benefit not only of ourselves but of our clients whose lives more often than not were made terribly difficult by the punitive, bureaucratic system that purported to serve them. Many of us were recent college graduates who had come of age sitting-in at lunch counters in the South, picketing Woolworth's in the North. The inner divisions which would disturb, enrage, sadden, and educate us in the antiwar, civil rights, and women's movements were not yet upon us. We knew which side we were on and believed we would pretty quickly overcome.

During the early days of those explosive social movements, after I quit my job at the Department of Welfare, I began teaching in a New York City high school where my students were only three or four years younger than me. The daughter of a working-class, immigrant father, I was motivated by the salary and benefits, as well as by my love of literature. But also, the destruction of the American Communist Party had left me with a visceral resistance to many forms of organized political action and in teaching I sensed the opportunity for social activism congenial with my temperament, history, and needs.

From that time I remember three small incidents that suggest the complexity of racial experience now so conscious in my life. I still believed that claiming a blindness to color could actually make you blind, that if people only treated each other as equals, centuries of history could be dismissed, even erased. I knew very little about American history, if knowing includes, as I now understand it does, the impact of African American history on the economic, political, artistic, and spiritual development of the United States. *Race Matters,* Cornel West assures us in the title of his collection of essays. *Black Matters,* Toni Morrison instructs

in one of hers. But I was assuring myself I was blind to color and failing
to see where the true blindness lay.

Each morning in the fall of 1966, I walk ten blocks downtown from my
apartment to Brandeis High School on 84th Street to meet my Academic
English class with whom I have developed a warm and easy relationship.
There are two girls in the class who are especially engaged and interested.
They sit in the front row, answer questions quickly and thoughtfully,
look at me with such lively response that I often find myself staring
intensely into their eyes while I teach. Outside of school, we are becoming friends. They have been to my apartment for dinner, met Douglas,
who I am engaged to marry. They have joined in his teasing of my "tired
black skirt" which I wear proudly, schooled in the bohemian values of
Greenwich Village and the High School of Music and Art. The more
worn and used-looking it becomes, the happier I am. But though its
slightly ratty, nubbed wool is a symbol of political pride for me, I am a
raggedy mystery to the foxy girls of late 1960s Harlem. Perhaps our
good-humored teasing about small cultural differences, and our close-
ness in age, helped me with no prior experience to teach them and my
other pupils about formal English grammar, which had always intrigued
me, and about reading novels and poetry, which were as crucial as food
to me and which I was determined, some day, to write myself.

During one lesson, referring to my particular class, a large number of
whom have not done their homework that day, I refer to them as "you
people." "You people have to do this work if you want to learn to write
better," I say, or something like that. Their faces turn to stone. Eyes move
instantly away from mine. Mild, muffled curses are heard. The two girls I
count as friends close their books and when I ask why, as the period has
not ended, they pretend innocence. "The bell's gonna ring any minute,"
one of them says with cold formality.

I am dumbfounded and confused, blind to my whiteness which now
shines from me like an unwelcome strobe light overheating the room. It
has never been gone, of course, not to my students, but only softened,
toned down to an unintrusive shine while real friendship and affection

grew. I was not wrong in sensing the development of trust; it was the fragility of the connection that I had underestimated. Despite my Jewish heritage which had made me familiar with the details of outsidedness, my olive skin and dark hair which caused me to be mistaken for a "Puerto Rican" almost daily, picket lines and rock-hard faith in our ability to overcome notwithstanding, there was an understanding of the nature of American society evident to my students that was still heavily veiled for me.

After class, I described my experience to Douglas who explained in one sentence: "When you said 'you people' they thought you meant Black people, and they assumed you meant it derisively, as in *you people never learn.*"

"But I didn't mean it that way at all," I explained. "I meant you people — in this class."

"It doesn't matter what you meant," I remember him telling me. I was convinced by his interpretation but deaf to his deeper warning. *It doesn't matter what you meant* when you are moving against a tide of history and social reality far more important than one white person's mistake. A white American either accepts the weight of this history or relinquishes the respect and possibility of authentic connection to Black Americans.

This memory might seem quaint now in an age of supposed ultra-consciousness about race. Or it might be buried altogether, if it were not for the fact that I encounter exactly the same sorts of mistakes in my white friends, students, colleagues, even at times in myself, all the time. The mistake is followed quickly by a denial of its importance, as if language itself, individual words and sounds, did not have a history thick with hidden meanings not to be casually undone.

I am hearing a story about common, everyday racism from one of my sons. It is a prototypical story of young Black maleness in an American city, 1990s. Khary's friend has rung the bell one night and is waiting for him to come downstairs. The friend, also Black and nineteen years old, drives the family car, a Toyota. We live on a racially mixed street in a racially mixed neighborhood, yet when Khary comes downstairs, he finds three cops surrounding his friend who is spread-eagle on the front of the car, being searched. Suspecting he had stolen the car, the cops approached him while he was standing against it, and when he objected, turned him around roughly and began their search. I am outraged and shout: "But this is unbelievable!" "Unbelievable?" my son says angrily. "Unbelievable, Mom? It happens to me all the time. If I'm not searched I'm still stopped and questioned, whenever I'm driving a decent-looking car." "It was just a word, a manner of speaking," I insist weakly. Because I already see that neither Douglas nor any other Black person would ever respond with that particular word. It is a small failure on my part, easily forgotten; but it signifies the vast space of white blindness to the dailiness of racism. My son feels that anxiety every time he steps out onto the street. I forget, am privileged to remain innocent.

My ignorance in this case can stand for the broader and deeper ignorance of many white Americans. The shock on their faces when they hear of Douglas's experience on a major highway: he is driving with his son and they are stopped by highway patrol, told to put their hands on the dashboard, cops' hands already on their guns. He has been speeding, they say, although he has not; they search his car, obviously looking for drugs, and only later, when he identifies himself as a government official in New York do they acknowledge that he was doing fifty-eight in a fifty-five mile per hour zone. Providence, Rhode Island, 1993.

The recurring story of young Black women students in white colleges across the country who are subjected to racial and sexual epithets hurled by white male students, so that a system of protection by Black male students has to be initiated to make them feel safe — a story of which most white Americans remain ruthlessly unaware.

Statistics about poverty and especially crime, about the crisis in urban education throughout the country — these realities of modern life are "known" and just as easily "forgotten," the forgetting aided and encouraged by media depictions of "inner city" (Black) children and teenagers as violent, usually orphaned or parented by drug addicts, a generation typically described as having no moral convictions, no sense of connection to society. With this illusion giving us cruel comfort, we can avoid concern, let alone action on behalf of these children.

Several years ago a well-known progressive private school in New York City distributed a questionnaire among its parent body asking for responses to common racial issues that arose year after year. Large percentages of parents, answering anonymously, responded that yes, they encouraged mixed race friendships among the students; yes, they supported extensive scholarships directed to Latinos and African Americans in order to integrate the school; but no, by a large majority, something near 90 percent, they would not be comfortable with interracial dating. When these figures are made public, the parent body in large numbers proclaim their astonishment. None of them can imagine who among them would feel in this way. They claim innocence of their own prejudices and, even after being presented with statistics, deny the obvious reality which would break down their illusions about themselves. The words of my student echo in my ear: *Slavery was always back then. Racism was always out there.* "It is the innocence," wrote James Baldwin in *The Fire Next Time*, "which constitutes the crime."

Last semester, in a class on African American autobiography and autobiographical writing in which we were discussing, among other themes, the whiteness of whiteness, several white students made the complaint that they were exhausted with talking about race, race, race. This, after half of one semester. The only Black woman student in the class in an overwhelmingly white college countered: "It is exhausting *being* a Black person in this school." I believe it was not the study of race or an introduction to Blackness, but the requirement to think about whiteness that tired them so. The autobiographical project, as the Black student suggested, is far more exhausting than the safer, more distant study of other people's lives.

I have heard numerous white colleagues and friends insist as well that they do not experience whiteness at all, because they are Jewish, or working class, or simply an outsider by personal temperament, as if awareness of skin color privilege might threaten the validity of equally real constraints. I am not a white person, I have heard white people say. I am a writer — a teacher — a woman — a shy and insecure man.

In 1967, a person who defined myself as straightforward and direct about all things, I returned to my class and boldly explained my intended meaning, apologizing for my insensitivity. I was back on track with the class, if I remember correctly, but I am aware that time and desire can replace the grimmer facts of history with pleasing illusions. It would be years, when I had birthed and raised Black children myself, been a disguised witness to white racism and that special form of American unconsciousness that tries to pass for tolerance, before I would really understand the more ominous truth packed at the bottom of Douglas's words: *It doesn't matter what you meant.*

A second memory: Out of my five daily classes, one by chance is all Black, no light-skinned, straight-haired Latinos, no whites. On the first day of the term, I am struck by my inability to see differences. I look at the faces and, exactly like the clichés of racism I have found contemptible all my life, they all look the same to me, like haunting replications in a dream. I fear I will never learn their names, distinguish their work one from the other. I can recall vividly, even all these years later, the sea of "black" faces looking up at me from their seats, the feeling of looking back at them and seeing no difference.

By the time a week has passed, this visual distortion will begin to break apart. I will have learned their names, heard their voices, seen their writing. In a month's time, I will begin to know which students are talented and capable readers and writers, which are uncomfortable with the written word, which are so frightened of and used to failure they don't know if they can write or not. By then I will also come to see a wide variety of skin tones, differences in weight and shape, distinctive lines and turns of flesh and feature, texture and style of hair. And I will not be able to imagine how these thirty-five students had looked so similar to me. I will notice Mitchell's long, loose curls fall over his brow, while James's tight, tiny curls appear almost solid from a distance, a soft cap of black. I will mark Francine's unusually large eyes, completely different from Althea's tiny round ones, their large black pupils leaving only quarter-moon slivers of white.

I have taught all-white, majority Latino, and mixed classes since then.

I know the feeling of indistinguishable mass that confronts any teacher on the first day. I also know that all people homogenize other physical types unfamiliar to themselves. Douglas's parents insisted my sister's hair and mine were "exactly the same color" when we first met, although in my family her "blond" hair was mythologized in its contrast to my dark brown. But I am remembering against the background of history: slavery, Jim Crow laws, segregation, and contemporary forms of racism; the degradation of depersonalization, the humiliation of invisibility. What unhinges me all these years later is the memory of not seeing obvious differences between black hair and brown, between curly, kinky, straight, or wavy. I did not see the broad-nosed, thin-lipped Gloria and narrow-nosed, dark-eyed Melinda with her full, sensuous lips. I did not see the rich color changes from a tan lighter than my own olive skin tones, to the medium brown of Douglas's skin, to the dark earth brown faces and hands, creases around the mouth and eyes, in knuckles and palms, folding into black. My actual vision was impaired. I saw a roomful of "black faces" on people who had only occasionally, distantly, or superficially come into my life. I have never forgotten that illusion of sameness and the white background against which it took its deceptive shape.

The third memory: It is spring 1968 — the weeks of the Columbia University Students' Strike. I have been teaching at Brandeis High School for two years now, and I am accepted as a friend and supporter of my students. One or two other white teachers are as well, but in this vast urban school we are a minority among one hundred or more. As the Columbia strike gains momentum, the passion for justice and principled action pours over into the high schools. Students protest, make demands, raise questions about school politics, faculty policies, curriculum. One day, H. Rap Brown, an outspoken leader of the Student Non-Violent Coordinating Committee (SNCC), appears on 84th Street with a megaphone, calling for students to come out into the streets. And they do. In large numbers, they leave their history classes, their home rooms, the gym, the cafeteria, and crowd onto the sidewalks, first marching through the halls chanting and shouting. Several of the student leaders are in my English class where, between our required Emily Dickinson and Shakespeare, we have been discussing Langston Hughes's question — "What happens to a dream deferred?"[4] They smile at me proudly, fists raised as they pass my room, and their pride is no match for mine.

Most of the white teachers lock themselves in their rooms, afraid of attack. This is a long time before guns will become prevalent in city schools. Perhaps there is an occasional switch blade, but these are generally kept out of sight. When one is used, in the yard or outside school grounds, it is an incident which provokes remarkable outrage and alarm, not the paralyzing genocidal resignation or punitive denunciation which is the more common response to Black teenage violence today.

With several other teachers, white and Black, I follow my students onto the streets. This is what my childhood, spirited by a belief in the Good Fight and the people's right to a voice, has prepared me for. The people are rising up, and they are my students. I am elated by the incomparable energy of collective action, an energy I will recognize in Meridel LeSeuer's essay, "I Was Marching": "I feel most alive, and yet for the first time in my life I do not feel myself as separate."[5] Embraced by that sense of belonging, I am literally *enlightened* — given clarity and vision by my students' voices, their passionate, hopeful, angry, released voices.

Hundreds of them crowd around the makeshift stage Rap Brown has erected on the street. He speaks to them of freedom, of Black being beautiful. Hell no, he tells them, we won't go to Vietnam and kill other people of color. We applaud. We raise our fists. Then he shouts, "Turn against your oppressors," and something like, "Go back into that school and teach your honkey teachers something they need to learn."

I am terrified. Suddenly I am afraid of all the students I don't know. I am taken over by a lifelong excessive fear of violence, and by the pain of sudden exile. I am way outside the world of "my people" and the fear moves through my body, rising into my face, which feels hot and dark red.

One of my favorite students is standing next to me. Recently, he has renamed himself Micar Sunyatta. Douglas and I went to court with him so he could do it officially. "Where are you from?" the white judge had asked. "Africa," the former Philip replied. "How long have you been here?" asked the judge. "All my natural life," answered the proud, sixteen-year-old, soon-to-be-Micar.

On the street, when he sees my skin go red, my eyes narrow with pain, as Rap Brown repeats his exhortation to students to confront their honkey teachers, and the students, who will do nothing violent this day, respond with cheers and shouts, he puts a lanky arm around my shoulders and says, "Hey, he doesn't mean you, nigger."

I am cool again, and for an illusory, calming moment, I think I am released back into the crowd's collective identity as I lean into Micar's shoulder surrounded by his protective arm. Maybe, I think, I have earned my stripes. But these particular stripes — black shadows on the white background of my permanently privileged skin — will have to be earned over and over again as I begin to live in a Black world as much as a white one. There is a lifetime of earning ahead, an alteration in vision and perspective about to happen very slowly, and I am only at the earliest stage. It will be years before I understand, from my own children's daily lives in an often hostile, sometimes terrifying and dangerous white world, that this is as it should be.

All this is not to say I won't be hurt and offended when I am rejected or insulted by Black people. When the Black students at the law school Douglas will soon attend regard me with disapproval and even in some cases outright dislike, when some of them don't want me to sit at the "Black table" in the cafeteria where I often go to meet Douglas after his classes, I will smolder with indignation and I will fight with them. A few will become close friends, and over the years will explain the bottomless well of suspicion and hurt turned to rage and anger that permeates Black American life. A Black friend who is a professor at a law school will talk to me about his loneliness, how the largely white faculty treat him politely but never comfortably, let alone intimately, even after twenty-five years. Douglas's family will explain, over dinners in restaurants, in hospital waiting rooms, before parent-teacher conferences, during visits down South, about the predictable ordinariness of racial insults. I will be surprised and embarrassed, then angry and ashamed, when I am asked repeatedly to step out into the street to get a cab when I am with Douglas, his brothers, later my own sons.

My children will pass through adolescence and, no longer easily protected, they will explain again — how it is to be Black, how whiteness feels to them, how race and color are constant, recurring, disharmonious drum beats behind every ordinary experience. I will see Douglas, at the age of fifty, anticipate a job interview with a special nervousness when the institutions interested in him are white, the interviewers all white men. I will see the pain on my sons' faces when, at a gathering of their white family, several people express anguish over the brutal killing of a young white American woman in South Africa — an anguish we all feel — but never refer to the thousands of Black deaths with the same anguish.

All through the years I will marvel at the ordinary, everyday generosity and patience on the part of so many Black people; that so many are willing to explain so often whenever there is a receptive ear, a genuine questioning. In the African American autobiography class, the young woman who describes her life at a white college as "exhausting" nevertheless explains again and again, and at length, what it feels like for her to be Black in America. The only other Black student in the class, a young man, will tell the stories of his life, coming of age and wanting simply to feel human, never able to feel anything but Black. In a prose poem spoken to the class, he writes: "I don't want to be / your angry niggah today — / I am two men / Human. And Hue Man."[6]

"I want to identify with your story," he will tell a white woman who has written a moving memoir about disappointment with her father's distance from her. "I see that your emotion is real, and I want to feel it too," he will say. "But I can't. I have no room for those kinds of angers. I am angry at racism. I am angry at slavery. I am angry that some place inside I still believe I am not as good as you."

It is one of those moments when I wish I were a Black teacher teaching Black literature. Just as there are times when, in spite of my convictions about the falseness of racial categories, about the human capacity to understand the experiences of another and the true value of a complex identity, I wish I could become Black for my sons.

I look at my student, trying by my facial expression to indicate support, admiration, and affection. Then I look at the white student and raise my eyebrows, trying to convey: Did you hear that? Were you listening carefully? Do you see how important this moment is? What I want her to hear is the never-ending constraint on his life; to see him, a person in many ways like herself, in the same college, another of the strongest students in the class, yet subject to perpetual battles of which her life is free. I want her to feel his words explode and disperse the blinding whiteness of whiteness.

It seems to me that anything I say aloud will break the solid weight of the silence, diminishing the moment with an abstracted, distancing analysis. But if I were Black, I could at least mitigate the pain on his face by taking some of it onto myself: I feel that way too at times, I might say; we all do, even the most successful of us. I settle for invoking the words of the many writers we have read who speak of the same pain, and the class ends on that note.

As I sit there watching them file out of the room, I know for certain that my white student, who has written brave and honest pieces all term, has been changed by the moment which has just passed. She has experienced what Emily Dickinson called a "conversion of the mind." I have seen it in her face, and in the weeks to come I will read it in her prose. The young Black man has been generous, self-revealing, but I fear the moment has not been useful for him. Perhaps it even caused him pointless pain. I think of all the times I felt white, powerfully white, obliviously white, visibly white, shamefully white: seeing a policeman come toward me at night and feeling the relief of his protection; walking into a country store in a strange town with no sense of anxiety that I might frighten the owner; speaking up for my outspoken mother-in-law when we are stymied by white institutions and she thinks my whiteness might more quickly get us what we want; feeling myself at the center when scholars talk about "women's history" and "women's rights;" planning my life, all of my life, constructing my dreams, without taking race into consideration at all.

Pressure increases until my head aches. Sitting at my desk in the now empty classroom I find I am imagining myself in the solitude of my apartment, or riding in a car, or walking on a secluded beach alone with Douglas and my children, and in a small way I understand the brutal pressure of color consciousness Blacks experience every public moment of their lives. I think about putting Adam and Khary to sleep when they were small, talking to them now, when they are home for a time, sitting in a softly lit room and speaking of unimportant or private things, intimate and personal moments when the world retreats from our door.

I was not a "white" mother when they were born, when they began to smile, speak, walk on their own. Nor were they "Black" nor even primarily sons when they first walked to school alone, wept at a failure or a prize denied, when one of them was called fat by another kid in the second grade. They were simply my children. When they first emerged from my body, our skins were the same shade of tan, and although when she saw Adam in the first moment of his life, my mother-in-law mentioned to me that he would "darken," I was ignorant, then, of African American attitudes toward differences in skin color and must have looked at her with an odd, confused smile. It would have seemed anachronistic, in those early years, to say to myself: Here is my Black son. When the white nurse, who knew Adam's father was Black, brought him to me crying for milk and said, "Oh, this one's a militant, a little Black Panther!" (because at the time the Panthers were active in New Haven where we lived) I felt a mixture of indignation and surprise at this first labeling by whites of my child as *other.*

This would be my first in a series of coming-of-age experiences related to race consciousness. My innocence broke down further when my four-year-old child was called *nigger* on a Fire Island beach, a New York community famous for its supposed liberality; when my teenage sons began to fear the police as much as I feared the crime of the city streets;

when many white teachers found their assertive questioning and intellectual passions to be "aggressive" and "intimidating," then denied all consciousness of racial difference, their callously held illusions a function of their casual entitlement and related refusal to see.

Shortly after Adam's birth when Douglas's parents moved to New York from the South and I became close to them, I was astonished to learn that in the Black world, everyone spoke about race all the time. Whites were always identified in stories about history and daily life. I remember the slight auditory shock—like earth shifting, or a sudden change in ocean current—when individuals were identified as "white" while Black was the unspoken assumption, rather than the other way around. Other Blacks were described by carefully observed differences in skin color. "She's a brown-skinned woman," I would hear Lois or Frederick, my father-in-law, say; "He's light-skinned, looks almost white"; "She's yellow (yalla) as me"; "He's black, I mean *black,* honey." As surely as if I had traveled thousands of miles from home, I entered a new world where small and large differences confused, entranced, irritated, and fascinated me.

I liked long hair on my children and let their curls grow out, brushing them back from their foreheads once a day, trimming the edges myself when the wild and beautiful mass became unruly or, in the summer, too hot. Lois was horrified by my hairdressing techniques. In the South, Black mothers carefully combed, braided, "fixed" girls' hair, cut boys' hair close to the scalp, flattening and taming kinky curls.

"Why don't you ever fix their hair?" Lois would say. "I do fix their hair," I'd insist, thinking of my long, careful brushing until their heads seemed surrounded by an electrified halo, golden highlights dazzling in the dark brown. We understood each others' speech well enough, but our miscommunications in the early years were as dramatic as those between my father, with his thick Yiddish accent, and Frederick, with his strong southern drawl. Liking each other for many reasons, including the love of a shared grandson, their conversations, nevertheless, were often reduced to a series of *whats?* and *I beg your pardons.*

"Lord," Lois would mutter, resigned to my inexplicable tastes in hairdressing, or thinking me just plain crazy. But I had always been called crazy by my own family for my rebellious ways, and sometimes Lois called me crazy when she meant to compliment me — if, for instance, ignoring politeness, I spoke thoughts out loud she considered *truth*. So I kept "fixing" the boys' hair as I liked until they grew older and demanded professional shaping and tamed curls themselves. Meanwhile, shared qualities deeper by far than fashion preferences would draw Lois and me together into a friendship as binding as any I have known.

Assumptions completely different from the immigrant Jewish patterns I had been raised with determined behavior in the kitchen and at the dinner table. I learned — and very quickly — to stop reaching into serving dishes for a pre-dinner bite of macaroni or meat, as the Jews I knew often did, behavior which is unthinkable in most Black homes I have visited. At the same time, Douglas was learning to tolerate my sister and cousins reaching with their fingers into bowls from which he, to his horror, was also expected to take his food.

Serious expressions of love bumped up against personal histories of sometimes hilarious disparity. When a cousin who was then very close to the family insulted me because I was Jewish and I wept at Lois's and Frederick's kitchen table, Frederick took my side immediately, then advised me to call her up and threaten to beat the shit out of her. We could meet in Central Park, he suggested, and I could whip her behind. My eyes widened in terror until a more realistic Lois comforted me with a pat on the shoulder saying, "Don't worry, honey, we know who would be whipping whose behind."

This was a time in my life when I learned more than in any other comparable period I can remember. There were the names of a dozen uncles and aunts and their offspring to memorize; all the inhabitants of Mitchell Wooten Courts, the project where Douglas and his siblings had been raised; Diddy, who helped Lois, a girl of sixteen when she had her first child, learn motherhood; Aunt Marie, the matriarch of the family, a young teenager when her parents were both dead, who with the help of two older brothers raised four younger siblings; the Harlem Inn Cafe, owned by Uncle Fulton, where Douglas and his brothers cooked and washed dishes during high school years; the first sit-ins and picket lines in town, organized by Simeon, my brother-in-law; the first time they all went to jail for civil rights activity in 1961; all the family lore through which issues of race and racism were threaded like the defining colors of a tightly woven tweed.

With a new baby to care for, I was delighted to spend long afternoons "lounging around the apartment" — as Lois called her steady stream of housework, watching soap operas on the always-turned-on television, smelling the elaborate dinners cooking all day on the stove. And during those long days which patterned recurringly into my years in graduate school, then as I began to work as a free-lance writer, I heard for the first time the family stories I would hear told and retold in decades to come, stories which by now have fired my children's imaginations as well as my own.

I felt completely accepted by Douglas's family, and this was aided, I was later told, by my family's welcoming of them, suggesting a genuineness in my capacity to love their son, which was not automatically assumed, to say the least, of white girls dating, in love with, or marrying Blacks. Despite the welcome, of course, I was and would always be white.

Some of this intractable definition is primarily cultural, much like the endless teachings by extended families to in-laws in any intermarriage. My cousin married a first-generation Italian American man, and in one way and another was reminded by his parents and siblings for years that she was Jewish. And I am certain that not one of our family's annual Seders has passed in twenty-five years without him being teased about his early confusion of gefilte fish with matzoh balls. In the same way, I have been introduced to water corn bread at least a dozen times, and only last month was offered regular corn bread at a family meal because it was assumed that I would not be able to tolerate the taste of the more "down home" variety. (Indeed, writing these words, I pause to call Lois and check the name of that particular bread, asking about its ingredients. "You can't cook this kind of corn bread," she tells me abruptly. "You won't like it, and I know you can't cook it." "Don't worry, Lois," I tell her.

"I don't want to cook it. I just want to write about it," — a reminder of our differences, now weighted so much less heavily than our shared history, it makes us both laugh.)

But there are also crucial distinctions between a Jewish woman becoming part of an Italian family, an Irish man marrying into a Jewish one, even a white American of any ethnicity marrying a Nigerian or Jamaican, and a white American marrying an African American. It is a function of racism, the special white American fear and suspicion of American Blacks, that most whites simply have no idea how different African American life is from their own. Its variation, for one thing, is frequently obliterated in assumptions that all Blacks think or feel the same way about everything from politics to personal relationships.

Language spoken, implied, expressed in a complex system of references, movements, sounds (there must be dozens of significant meanings to the sound mmm, hmmm) is misunderstood as radically as a speaker of English might misunderstand French, remembering only key words and phrases from high school language classes but missing connotation and sense. And it is no mystery that so many young white people are attracted to "Black English" generation after generation. It possesses the same complex and subtle revelations of human feeling as jazz, and although I have often winced at whites' imitations of Black language, I have been tempted to such appropriation myself, just because the words are so perfect, the tone — which I can never get quite right — so meaningful. I might say "cut" off the light, and "pull" off your coat, after twenty-seven years of living with Douglas, but I wish I could say "shiiiit" in exactly his tone of mockery, or "say what?" in response to some outrageous remark in the way his brother Ricky used to do. "Ain't studdin' her," Lois will say of some person whose opinion she disrespects to say the least, but I have never been able to get it to come out quite right, any more than Douglas, even after all these years, can say *chutzpah* without the gutteral *ch* sounding like a soft, simple *h*.

Few whites are educated or sophisticated about the rich meanings and history of African American music. I had hardly listened to jazz at all when I was in my twenties, knew only a few of the most common spirituals and blues. I certainly had no idea of the complex narrative and spiritual functions of music in African American life.

As to African American history, which of course I had learned nothing of in school, I knew only the names the Communists valorized: Harriet Tubman, Frederick Douglass, Langston Hughes, W. E. B. Du Bois, and of course Paul Robeson. Better than nothing, but not really very much at all.

Since his late teens, my father-in-law, Frederick, had been a professional gambler. Through the combination of a brilliant mathematical memory (he could memorize the order of a deck of cards in minutes) and a complex system of cheating, which he described without fanfare as a financial necessity, he had been able to support three sons, a daughter, a wife, and himself and see all the children through college. His earnings were sufficient for Lois not to have to work, and this piece of family history, that neither parent had been forced to work for whites since their early teens, was considered a possible explanation for their relative lack of bitterness toward whites in general, although on an individual basis they were as adept at spotting, denouncing, and analyzing all forms of racism as any Black person I have ever met. This interpretation was a revelation to me, but was so obvious to the family I don't think anyone had put it into words until I asked. Douglas was exposed to an equally new world of Jewish culture, of course, but I was also learning how it felt to see the world from a Black perspective for the first time, while he already understood the white one in all its oppressive and often villainous detail.

Soon I began to hear, to notice, innumerable racist remarks when I was on my own, away from my family, and to understand that I would have to protect my children from cruelty and callousness in many situations. When the boys were about three and seven years old, a great aunt, pointing to Khary in a roomful of people, declared — That one's prettier, he's lighter. White friends would repeatedly refer to the trusting good nature of rural Americans. One example often given in evidence of this was the custom of vegetables placed on tables along country roads, a can for payment nearby but with no person present to oversee the transaction. "People are so friendly here," I would be told. "They just assume you are a good person." And I'd think, not if my children jumped out to get that corn in this all-white town.

I began to relinquish a sense of comfort and belonging whites everywhere unconsciously assume. When the family made a trip to North Carolina by car, food in large quantities was packed into baskets, along with washcloths, towels, and all the necessary tools for eating. Legal segregation, in 1972, had ended only recently and no one wanted to risk being insulted, perhaps turned away at restaurants or motels along the route south. Hearing the family discuss these matters with my small son in the car, I thought, as most parents always do, that the conversation would pass over his head unheeded. But he was learning lessons as I was. When he made a trip to New Orleans with his father years later, and the car broke down in Tennessee, he was so terrified he became ill for days.

We believed it was absolutely necessary to live in a racially mixed neighborhood (of which there are few in New York, almost none in most of the rest of the country), and I was disappointed by how rarely white friends felt the same way. Although I know many whites who parent Black children do not grasp this seemingly obvious fact, I saw I would have to take race into consideration in every decision I made about their lives, from the choice of doctor and dentist, to evaluations of teachers in school. I learned this simply by observing and listening to what Black people did and said. I came to understand, for example, that I had better make myself highly visible to their mostly white teachers hoping to mitigate their opinions about Black children being uncared for and unruly. When the teachers saw a white, middle-class mother, I incurred the privileges of caste and class many whites regularly and unconsciously enjoy. "Go on and use it, you've got to protect them any way you can," Lois told me when, in the privacy of her kitchen, I confessed my sense of shame. Her permission eased but did not, I am glad to say, obliterate the guilt I sensed it was better to feel than to sweep away in a fog of psychological cliché.

Guilt can of course be a destructive emotion; fired by hostility and moral righteousness, it can paralyze, alienate, even turn real contrition to anger and hate. But I also recall hearing the words of Primo Levi, speaking about the Nazi past, saying that guilt is the emotion felt by decent people when they are witness to terrible injustice they can do or have done nothing about.[7]

My sons are in their early twenties now, gone off into their own lives. When I see them together, besides being struck by the usual maternal affections and sentiments, I see two young Black men who, like many other African Americans, encompass ethnic mixtures not visible to the racial polarizations of the typical American eye, and it is impossible not to marvel at the generational continuities which transcend in their mystery even the mystery of genes. I see the visual echo of my mother's broad, Jewish mouth on Adam's face, but I also hear the early dissonant tones of his saxophone and guitar, now become soulful melody and harmonious chord, and I believe his love of music may have taken form during the many days he spent lying on the rug in his grandparents' home, listening with Frederick for hours to Otis Redding, Duke Ellington, Ella Fitzgerald, and John Coltrane. When Khary raises his eyebrows it is as if Lois's brows were painted on his forehead, but in his political activism it is impossible not to recognize his Jewish grandfather, as fierce in his convictions and pure in his dedication as his grandson is now. Walking down the street recently, a son on each side, I felt the familiar paradox between reality and appearance. Passersby would wonder at our connection, fail to see our resemblances, never imagine those vital cells far beneath the surface of our skins where we have changed and created each other.

By the time my children were well into their elementary school years, I had begun to feel where once I was anaesthetized. As a Black friend of mine put it, everything at times seemed to be about race. Like a woman with a bone knocked out of joint, or an immigrant who is estranged from her country of origin yet does not really belong to her new home, I was aware of nothing so much as dislocation.

"White bitch," a young girl says to me in the street when I accidentally bump her arm with a heavy bag. I feel mixed emotions — angry at her rudeness, but also at the highly racialized society that makes this particular epithet meaningful to her. Displaced somewhere between American Blackness and American whiteness, I stop still on the street and for a moment can't remember where I am going.

"Of course your children got into those colleges, they're Black," I am told by several white acquaintances when Adam and Khary are admitted to Ivy League schools. "It's amazing how articulate he is," a fellow teacher says of a Black student who, like many others in his generation, dresses in loose jeans and high-tops; "I'd never think he was so bright." "Come on," one white woman insists to me, "You have to admit you are afraid of large groups of Black boys on the street when they're being loud, their baseball caps turned around, their jeans down to their knees."

I walk onto a desolate subway platform or down a dark street and see such a group, and I *am* somewhat anxious, as most women are. I see the images of tough and dangerous adolescent males the media has taught us to fear. But I also see my sons and their friends, gentle boys who might look exactly the same as these boys, and I am afraid for them as much as of them. I think about being a woman in the city at a time when male violence has been increasing and increasingly valorized all over the world. I think of being a woman. I think of what Reaganism has done to American cities including the city I used to love. I do not think exclusively of race.

"But you must see that they're Black," the white woman says. Of course I do see that they are Black; it is the meaning of Blackness that has deepened and changed. Now I feel the more disturbing dislocation of the voluntary exile. I remember exactly who I am and where I am headed, but my identity is hidden and with it the perspective I now hold. I wish she would see that I am no longer an ordinary white woman, and shut her mouth out of politeness or fear, the way she might do if I were Black.

The whiteness of whiteness is the blindness of willful innocence. It is being oblivious, out of ignorance or callousness or bigotry or fear, to the history and legacy of American slavery; to the generations of racial oppression continuing; to the repeated indignities experienced by Black

Americans every single day; to the African cultural heritage which influences every single American, long here and newly arrived; to the highly racialized society that this country remains. It is denying this fundamental national reality by insisting on Black culpability and pointing to Black superstars; by comparisons to other nonwhite Americans with profoundly different histories; by looking away from one's own skin color privilege and, in bell hook's words, "the way in which whiteness acts to terrorize";[8] by being too timid to face the role whites and whiteness have played and continue to play in the world.

No sooner have I become aware of my whiteness than I want to abandon all connection to it. In this doomed wish, however, I am stymied by the painful, almost continuous consciousness of lifelong, unearned, unjust privilege, and that burden is a reminder that it is far too early for me to give into the luxury of fatigue. Memory leads to consciousness, I remember telling my students, recollection to the possibility of meaning, which always reveals a responsibility to the world. The autobiographical attitude can result in a clarity of conscience that is hard to ignore.

And now, feeling inadequate more than impatient, I go on to describe for my white friend the intricate web of limiting possibility that almost all African Americans experience, a constraint which has gone on for 400 years. I want to tell her how it has destroyed, crippled, limited, or merely hurt millions upon millions of lives. When Douglas speaks to me about growing up Black, it is this sense of constraint he often refers to — the idea taking hold very early that he would probably not be all he was able to be. I know that Black adults, from family, to college professors, to mentors of every sort, are repeatedly telling my sons, along with other young Black people, that even now, in some ways especially now, they will have to try harder, be better, smarter, clearer, and more focused, in order to succeed at all.

Many people, of course, are subject to constraints by virtue of economic class, gender, sexual preference, disability, ethnicity. Any minute my white friend will tell me this. But there is a centuries-old system of constraint by skin color that persists in America and that we, as a nation, prefer to qualify, mitigate, euphemize, or completely ignore. It is a reality so frightening, apparently, that in many discussions about race you can count on a "yes but" phenomenon. Any reference to racial inequity will frequently be responded to by white people with statements such as: Yes, but what about sexism? Yes, but what about homophobia? Anti-Semitism? Racism against Asians, or the difficulty of any immigrant group first coming to these shores?

All these inequities exist, and it is important to find the substantive and structural commonalities among them, not to mention the overlaps in actual lives. But it is equally important to focus on the specific nature and history of racism against African Americans without instant dilution into wider categories. Even in the concept of multiculturalism, now revolutionizing the way we think and learn about nearly everything, there is a danger of not paying attention to this very particular American experience and in losing our attention, losing our heart.

As at every other point in this story of racial mixing that has so colored the central experiences of my life, my intellectual curiosity grew out of a personal maternal struggle: to better comprehend the lives of my sons. Yet that desire circled back again: through them I wanted to know the world beyond their stories, the life that surrounds and alters their lives.

I haven't dreamed again of being lost under the African sun, but I am a wanderer in most of my dreams, and in none that I can remember have I found my way home. This familiarity with outsiderness has served me well in my journey across the American color line. But perhaps there is a place I have not yet imagined where exiles and strangers gather, racial hybrids of consciousness which can run as thick as blood, who out of necessity make the effort to rename what it means to belong.

THREE.

PASSING OVER

I think the hard work of a non-racist sensibility is the boundary crossing, from a safe circle into wilderness; . . . to travel from the safe to the unsafe . . . This willing transgression of a line, which takes one into a new awareness, a secret, lonely and tabooed world — to survive the transgression is terrifying and addictive. To know that everything has changed and yet that nothing has changed; and in leaping the chasm of this impossible division of self, a discovery of the self surviving, still well, still strong, and, as a curious consequence, renewed. — *Patricia J. Williams,* The Alchemy of Race and Rights

I

I am looking in the mirror but this time I am not scanning my face for new wrinkles, not trying to get accustomed — ten years after the fact — to thinking of myself with grey hair. I am looking at my skin, focusing on color. It is summer and, as usual, my skin has darkened to a medium brown. I am darker than some of the "Black" people in my family. Even in the depths of winter, I am a yellowish tan, which during the worst sunless months of February and March seems horribly to verge on green. I use a bit of Blush-On to provide a pink otherwise absent from my flesh. Typical Jewish coloring — olive skin, once dark hair; a very similar color to Khary who, however, because of his hair and broadness of feature, is obviously Black, a few shades lighter than Adam and Douglas, who are also obviously Black.

Although any of us could be mistaken for Latino on New York City streets and often are. Khary told me the other day that Latinos are often annoyed with him if he cannot speak adequate Spanish, assuming he has abandoned his heritage. The same thing used to happen to me when I was a young brunette. This grey hair seems to mark me, though, despite skin tone and wide lips, as "white."

My father was blue-eyed; his fair skin burnt a crisp red in the sun. Although I always knew him as white-haired (like Adam, he began turning grey in his early twenties) his blondness found its genetic way into my sister's hair, which is a kind of mixture, now, of gold and silver framing intense blue eyes. Her skin, which is a pale beige with lovely pink highlights, like our father's turns a dangerous red in the sun. Her children, however, who in this way take after their swarthy Jewish father, are brown-skinned for white people. Various shades of beige to light brown, although according to American racial categories they are certainly *white*.

When I read the works of English writers who describe real or imaginary encounters with Africans, the sense of arrogant superiority is generally associated with being European. The "great" cultures of Europe are typically contrasted with the "primitive" or "underdeveloped" or, at worst, "savage" cultures of Africa. *Whiteness,* though, seems to be an American category, a way of contrasting oneself to people who are *not white*.

What if I stop thinking of myself as white, but rather as a Jewish American with an olive tan- to brown-colored skin? Suddenly, the whole complex pattern of skin color privilege takes on a quality of increased absurdity. It is clearly a false abstraction, given reality by history, the politics of domination by one group of people over another, nothing to do with anything intrinsic or physically real.

Stories of "passing" fill African American literature — Black people, usually women, passing for white in an attempt to find opportunity, economic advancement, some imagined internal freedom to be. Actual Black families include people who look white. Douglas has two great uncles, brothers, both of whom looked white, but only one chose to live among Blacks in the segregated town. All the nieces and nephews were taught never to address the "white uncle" as though they knew him, although they knew perfectly well he was the brother of Uncle Clyde who lived among them.

Mrs. Fuller, a close family friend whom I met on several occasions during our trips south, looked much "whiter" than I do. "We never really knew what Mrs. Fuller was," Lois told me. "Some people said she was Indian. Some people thought she was part white. But as long as she wanted to be Black that was okay with us."

As long as she wanted to be Black. "Blackness is and Blackness ain't," says the Preacher in the text of the Blackness of Blackness in the Prologue to *Invisible Man.* Whiteness, too, is and whiteness ain't. Where it is, there is a closed, socially recognizable circle. The circle, of course, is increasingly besieged as it must and should be. But it is still a large circle surrounded by strong walls, containing many of the economic privileges and social powers supposedly afforded by American society to all of its citizens. "Whiteness" is the sign of a privileged caste strengthened by centuries of an ideology of personal and cultural supremacy. White people, we are told, are "better" in almost everything from hair quality, to individual intelligence, to the "complexity" of our cultural and aesthetic histories.

And yet whiteness only exists because it needs to call itself superior to something else. If whiteness were to disappear, we would still be left with other forms of cultural conflict and religious hatred, of course. But other forms have an existence whiteness cannot claim. I am not white in the same way as I am Jewish or American. Those identities, however hyphenated or ambivalently claimed, denote language, history, food, humor, literature — any number of cultural productions. Yet *whiteness is,* and, paradoxically, it is learning the depth and dimension of my whiteness — which I can no more easily throw off than I can the social definitions of my gender — that leads to the realization that I am not really white at all.

Everything, it seems, about this subject of race is and at the same time ain't. Race itself is not biologically true, yet we have brought it into a polarized existence which cannot be denied. This true / untrue categorical conception affects all the ways we think about skin color and about history.

Reading this chapter to Khary in an early draft, he commented, "You are still using the perspective of a white person, Mom, when you call Sarah and Simon (my sister's children) brown. And when you talk about 'passing.' It's completely different for whites and for Blacks to talk about color, or about passing over to the other side. Very fair-skinned Black people might choose to leave the Black community, but they were never forced out. There have always been 'white' people in Black families. A fair-skinned Black leader, like Malcolm X, would not be respected less because of his skin color when he is so strongly identified as Black. There is a lot of color consciousness and color prejudice in the Black community, but its origin is in the white world."

Color colors our dreams. When fear of male violence enters my dreams, men with guns are white. They are beating down our doors, or jumping into the backs of cars, threatening our lives, forcing us to take them where they want to go.

In one of my classes in African American autobiography, I had a brown-skinned Dominican student who insisted right up to the last day of the term that we Americans polarized race in a way that was meaningless to her. "I am neither Black nor white," she insisted. "In the Dominican Republic we don't separate people that way." Yet, she wrote a powerful sketch about her parents and grandparents instructing her never to marry a Black man because their family was not *Black* — these brown-skinned people who were clearly not white insisted. And she can stand for many Latin and South Americans who insist there is no race consciousness in their countries where, nevertheless, the ruling and privileged classes are light skinned or white, the poor and often degraded classes, dark skinned or Black. There is even a category in Brazil, I have read, of "Honorary White," so that a visibly Black celebrity, Pélè, for instance, the champion soccer player, was able to "become white" — the sign of his fame, influence, and wealth.

Another student, the daughter of a white mother and Black father, confessed a story of mother-daughter estrangement. "My mother always told me I was the same as her," my student says, tears coming to her eyes. "What she meant was I was good enough to be white, even though I am obviously Black." She holds out slender, brown fingers for me to see, three of them nearly covered, knuckle to nail, in filagreed silver rings. "She never taught me anything about the great Black American traditions in the arts or in political resistance. By insisting I was 'just like her' she made me feel being Black was something to be ashamed of."

All this student's fiction is about daughters searching for fathers who are either imprisoned or dead. Her story is typical of many I have heard. It is too late for clichés about all of us being the same. Being the white mother of Black children in a racist society is a strenuous process, dangerous to oversimplify. One must be educated, willing to cross over into an entirely new way of seeing things.

I look in the mirror and see skin that is tan to medium brown. I look at my children and see skin that is tan to medium brown. But the other night, I was told by one of our building guards that some cops came to the door after Khary had walked out, on his way to the video store. They asked about him, if he lived in the building, what kind of person he was. They were looking for someone who "looked like him." For weeks I was frightened each time he went out in the street, night or day; that he might be arrested, "mistaken" for a criminal they were following. I wanted to follow him down the street, to his job, to his friends' houses, hiding behind him, ready to protect at a moment's notice, as I once did the first time he walked alone to school in the second grade. To deny the reality of Blackness can be literally psychotic or suicidal.

In a story called "The Kind of Light That Shines on Texas," by the African American writer Reginald McKnight, a young Black boy who is trying to understand the web of race, social identity, and self experiences an epiphany when he understands the paradoxical patterns of color in which he and every other American are caught.

> The light made my skin look orange, and I started thinking about what Wickham [his teacher] had told us once about light. She said that oranges and apples, leaves and flowers, the whole multicolored world, was not what it appeared to be. The colors we see, she said, look like they do only because of the light or ray that shines on them. "The color of the thing isn't what you see, but the light that's reflected off it." Then she shut out the lights and shone a white light lamp on a prism. We watched the pale splay of colors on the projector screen; some people oohed and aahed. Suddenly, she switched on a black light and the color of everything changed. The prism colors vanished, Wickham's arms were purple, the buttons of her dress were as orange as hot coals, rather than the blue they had been only seconds before. We were all very quiet. "Nothing," she said, after a while, "is really what it appears to be." I didn't really understand then. But as I stood at the window, gazing at my orange skin, I wondered what kind of light I could shine on Marvin, Oakley and me that would reveal us as the same.
>
> I sat down and stared at my arms. They were dark brown again.[1]

Color is and color ain't. It is into the uncompromising light of that consciousness that I journey through my sons' childhood and adolescent years. My memories of this passing over cover nearly ten years, from the time they began to turn into their own lives, at about twelve or thirteen, to their coming-of-age in their college years. It is not one of those journeys marked by a straight line from here to there. I experienced false starts, backward slides, new sources of fear and of pride as I came to understand the dramatic gifts and dangers of being Black in America. Slowly, I began to see my sons as part of a long, arduous and profoundly imaginative historical process: the struggle of Black Americans to create an identity out of dismemberment and oppression, to tell and write stories of recovery, creation and recreation, to actively engage the powerful emotional need of human beings to name themselves.

"Where is Africa America?" a character asks in *The Circle is Unbroken is a Hard Bop,* a play by the African American poet, Sekou Sundiata. "I don't know," the narrator answers. "I am making it up as I go along."[2]

Transition years. Passing over from one sort of being to another. A wider vision of things, not necessarily more inclusive, but more realistic, more clear.

"What is it like for you? How do you think about race these days? About being Jewish? About being Black?"

I ask my sons these questions repeatedly, trying, like a weaver of some complexly patterned cloth, not to lose a thread of reality. They do not only live in the world, after all. They are also individuals, with the individual's precious mystery of self-creation, never to be casually or finally explained.

One night, Adam spoke to me about the irrelevance to him of any external image or definition, who he might or should be in anyone else's view. He was nearly graduated from college, about to begin living on his own. "They can go to hell," he said, "with all their assumptions, expectations, and simplifications. Of course I am a Black person." He laughed slightly at the ludicrousness of questioning so obvious a reality. "But I am also Jewish." He holds his hands out in what seems, at the moment, to be a typically Jewish gesture, rocking slightly in the chair where, twenty-two years before, I had rocked him. Then he added, "And I'm a bit Italian too," because two of the closest adults from his childhood are Italian and they too have influenced his temperament, he believes, his language, and his vision of things. "What does it matter if they're not blood?"

I remember the essay he wrote on his college applications in which he described pride and gratitude in his mixed heritage — that it gave him just the ambiguously defined mixture of self he loved and felt comfortable with, a fluid, even uneasy identity a source of excitement to him. "If white people reject me," he said, "that's their problem. The world is full of mixed people and there's no such thing as 'race'—I know who I am."

As soon as he could talk, he began asserting himself, insisting on his own way and heading in his own direction the moment his legs were strong enough to get him there, his own council always the voice with greatest weight. Coaches, teachers, relatives, and friends—now casting directors, producers, and agents—none has the ability to throw him off balance, it seems, even when rejections are painful, evaluations poor, or luck bad. I have come to see this quality, handed down by Douglas's parents to their strongest children—a combination of optimism, endurance, and clarity of direction—as a virtue that enables them to survive. Douglas's capacity to be self-defined clearly enabled him to prevail over a childhood lived in complete legal segregation under the pervasive and humiliating Jim Crow laws that were in effect until his early manhood. The whiff of battle became more enticing than frightening. I have actually seen Adam and Douglas smile gleefully when they know some one or some group believes something about them that is wrong, and the time has come to fight. They gain determination by the very misinterpretations and false namings that would drive me to paralyzing rage and tears.

Khary has some of this quality as well, as I suppose any Black person who survives in this society must, but the night we talked about race and identity—the year he entered college—he emphasized other realities. For him, the need to belong was crucial, he said. People live more creatively and safely when they feel part of a group larger than themselves. As a young boy, he had tried continually to make sense of his racial and cultural heritage, and he reminded me of a poem he had written when he was twelve.

It was summer, and he was on a crowded bus, sitting next to an old woman. Her sleeves were rolled up, and as she turned her arm he saw numbers seared into her flesh, which he knew meant she was a concentration camp survivor. He looked at her face, feeling sympathy and kinship. (*I am in a world of my own / my emotions on a fragile string. / 1407–1B / Black lettering / Scarred tissue / Wounds my eyes.*) But she removed her arm, stared at him uncomfortably and eventually she rose and moved away from him, preferring to stand, he felt, than sit next to him. (*She can feel me / smell my stench / sense my precise presence.*) Perhaps, being young and vulnerable, he misread her discomfort and she was only afraid of being stared at. But it is very likely her more general feeling was affected by race.

He stared at her, at the number on her arm, screaming silently: *I am Jewish! / I am Jewish. / Can you not see through my brown skin?*

But she walked to the front of the bus, turned away from him. *My seat is left open,* he wrote, and then, the moment catapulting him from one sense of himself to another: *I am Black to the bone.*

I reread the poem with the pain of remembering other similar incidents which begin to suggest a pattern, its full meanings hidden from me until now.

Jewish friends in high school would inform him that he was "not really Jewish," and I would think about the skin color and ethnic diversity of Jews around the world, recalling a trip to Israel when we encountered brown-skinned Jews from various parts of Africa, including the Ethiopian Jews who were then new immigrants to Israel. I remember visiting a school where these recent arrivals were learning Hebrew, the children running up to surround Douglas, who was the only African American in our group, him taking them in his arms saying, "Shalom, Sugar. Shalom." But in the United States, most Jews are Ashkenazi, of European background, and like the members of my own extended family, they are white.

During Khary's second year of college, one of his visiting professors was embroiled in a controversy at his home institution for teaching the Nation of Islam pamphlet, *The Secret History of Blacks and Jews,* a work which implicates the Jews in the American slave trade. I went to a bookstore to find it and read it for myself. It is clear that some Jews participated in the slave trade and owned slaves, but reading the litany of hatred toward the Jews singled out as a people made me cringe in fear. I read through but could not buy the book. Echoes of Nazi rhetoric rang in my ears. I was not worried that my son would be turned into an anti-Semite, but even the fact that he was considering the arguments seriously deeply upset me. On the other hand, I felt strongly that the American Jewish community was singling out African American anti-Semitism in a racist way. The white Christian right seemed more of a threat to American Jews, if only because their power is so much greater than anyone's in the Black community. And too many Jewish communities and writers, even progressive Jews, concentrated on the evils of anti-Semitism in the Black community with no reciprocal concern about or acknowledgement of racism in the Jewish community. These complex issues generated a long correspondence and many discussions between Khary and myself including trying to describe how *Jewish* each of us felt. At one point, he explained his feelings this way:

"If I were walking along the street and someone was beating up Daniel [his oldest childhood friend] because he is Jewish, I would interfere because I would think — this is wrong. If I were walking down the street and someone was beating up a Black kid, I would interfere because I would think — this is me."

"Obviously," he said the night of our discussion, looking back at the knots of his own confusion and emerging awareness, "I can never fully belong to anyone but Black people. I feel connected to African culture, and to African American culture, and in some ways to Jewish culture. Just as friends of mine are connected to the cultures of Carribean mothers, in one case to a Yoruba father, in another to an Italian mother. But they all see themselves as Black people, and so do I."

The word *Black,* then, represents more than simply a shade of skin or shape of feature that suggests African or diasporan heritage. It is reminiscent, ironically, of the way many secular Jews feel about being Jewish: a sense of things, including a shared history and culture, a besieged status in society, and the strengths of collective knowledge hidden from the dominant group, a knowledge communicated in a glance, a touch on the shoulder, a phrase of music or language, a slap of the hand.

"But don't Blacks sometimes reject mixed or 'interracial' people as not being Black enough?" I asked. And I remember Adam being told by some Black children in elementary school that he was not really Black. He told us the story and began to cry. He talked about his music, how personally he responded to the emotional and political history of jazz and blues, how his Blackness, even at ten, eleven, twelve years old was a powerful, solid ground from which he listened to, played, and began to write music. How could these girls doubt him? Momentarily, he seemed thrown by the realization that others might be blind to the certainties he never questioned about himself.

Years later, when he was living and working as an actor in Los Angeles, he wrote me a letter in which he described it all this way:

> Notwithstanding my multi-cultural consciousness, my racial identity is simply that of a Black man as any other Black man of any combination. I am related to and I relate to others as a Black man. Sometimes, I identify with Jewish culture because of you and my Jewish family, but it is never without the footnote of knowing that I am perceived as a Black man who 'does a good Jew' instead of a Jew celebrating his own culture. Over the years of growing up, that phenomenon has pulled me further and further from a comfortable, natural identification with Jewish culture. I still retain some, but I am conscious of a different perspective on that part of me now as my age increases and my innocence decreases. When I am in a group of people who are white, Jewish or not, I am a Black man. When I am in a group of people who are Black, I am a Black man. I feel no difference in my identity because my mother is white and Jewish. I only feel, perhaps, a greater familiarity with white people than Blacks who have not been exposed to white family and friends. But that familiarity, or comfort, is not related to a sense of identity.[3]

Khary acknowledged witnessing Black rejection of "mixed race" students, but this happens, he believes, when they insist on being "mixed" — the white part seemingly offered as a sign of superiority. "If you consider yourself Black, whatever else you might be ethnically," he said, "it doesn't matter to anyone what other mixtures you have inside of you. You're still

Black, and you know it. And that's where I belong." In other words, you can be Asian, or Jewish, or Dominican, but you cannot be white if you're Black.

Khary's developing thought echoes a childhood temperament too. A shyer boy than his brother, a child who needed more attention, more caretaking, who took in the sorrows of the streets. During his early childhood, homelessness escalated until the streets of upper Broadway were filled with people lying in doorways, begging for money, sometimes dignified, sometimes desperate and scary, always in need. I asked him recently if he remembered that when he was five or six the streets were different. It was a more occasional event to encounter a beggar, sometimes not more often than once a day. He has no recollection of such a time.

Very early in his life, the inner and outer worlds conflate. His boundaries are more permeable than his father's and brother's; he takes the grief and dislocation around him into his emotional life, into his body, which is subject to a variety of ailments, into his dreams. Intimate partner of this vulnerability is anger and defensiveness in the world. He is described by several white teachers as a "kid with a chip on his shoulder." The chip grows stronger, fits more perfectly into his body over the years of coming of age in a city where suspicion of Black boys and men is increasing, becoming more cruel, where many stores in his neighborhood institute a system of bells and locked doors so that proprietors can determine whom to admit, whom to keep out, and those kept out are invariably people who look like him.

Always strongly linked to his surroundings, needing beautiful things and orderly rooms, playing with dolls and flowers long past the typical age for boys, he begins now to create his own hardness, while I watch with some sense of relief. (I realize this is a mother's story. Khary might focus everything differently. But I remember Douglas and Adam were in love with the world in its widest parameters, while Khary loved home.)

By the time he is ten, he is fundamentally political — that is, he finds in political action and analysis the path to personal and collective survival. He has learned, like Adam and Douglas, not to mind so much what people say of him, or so they all tell me though I find it very difficult to imagine let alone attain. But the need to belong is powerful in him, and he marks that belonging, as he moves through college life, in studies of African and African American history and literature, in a social life made up almost entirely of Black (though multi-ethnic) friends, and in taking a leadership position in the Black life of the college.

I do not mean to reduce political conviction to psychology any more than I would want to obscure personal stories in large generalities about social and political truths. But in the late 1980s and early 1990s, life in this country is as racialized as ever before. And like any other children, mine are coming of age in specific political times. "People are trapped in history," James Baldwin writes in "Stranger in the Village," "and history is trapped in them."[4]

In 1991, a notorious crime took place in New York City. A young woman, jogging around the reservoir in Central Park in the evening, was brutally beaten and raped, nearly killed by a large group of teenage boys. Her name was never released by the press, and she became known as the Central Park Jogger. A fairly large number of teenage Black boys were quickly rounded up, arrested, and questioned by police. Several of them were brought to trial. Of these, some were found guilty of the terrible act of violence. But the names of all the boys were printed daily, for many months, in our newspapers, and one of them had a name almost identical, except for one letter, to Khary, who was about their age at the time. One day, cleaning his room, I found a piece of writing about this case. The shared name was the occasion for his realization that perhaps he too might have been picked up and accused of rape and near murder, just because he too was a teenage Black boy. Why not? he asked on the page. He was frequently stopped by police and asked to identify himself though he was doing nothing suspicious or wrong. He was frequently "mistaken" for a mugger, a thief, a troublemaker of some kind. Some of these boys were mistakenly identified, or ultimately found not guilty, and yet their names too were read every day in searing headlines about "wild animals." Khary walked the streets during those weeks, as he does now, knowing he was being looked at, perhaps, by that taxi driver passing him by, by the storekeeper following him down the aisle, in the anxious glance of a woman crossing the street at twilight as he comes toward her, as a wild animal too. There but for the grace of God go I, he wrote.

At the time I was disturbed by his identification, wanting to diminish my fear of him coming to harm by insisting on definitive differences between my son and these other sons. But when I discussed my feelings with Black friends, especially those who were parents, they just raised their eyebrows and nodded vehemently in support of his reaction. I saw that I would have to come to see that other Kharey as my son too, whether he was one of the guilty or one of the falsely accused; in either case, he was a child whose personal, interior story was formed in part by the world in which we continue to allow him to exist. I must find the way to feel, in all of my whiteness, the connection my son understood in part by virtue of the color of his skin. The next week, in the same city, a poor Black woman was brutally raped then thrown from the top of a building. There was a small amount of coverage in the papers, hardly any publicity after a few days. When you are passing over, you encounter the pain of issues broader, if not deeper, than the love of your own individual child.

I want to keep hold of all the threads in this fabric of color and race, try not to lose an important piece. A white person, I am learning in the most intimate relationships what it means to be Black. A Jewish mother, I am watching my sons move farther and farther away from a sense of a Jewish identity and, although I am not religious at all, this leaves me feeling a specific kind of loneliness. I see all the colors I learned as a child-painter to include in rendering the true textures in human flesh — not only pinks and browns, but yellows, blues, dark red, even green; and I see also that Blackness, no matter how pale the skin, and whiteness, no matter how dark, can overwhelm the more truthful kind of color-making light that shines on us all.

Often, during the years of transition, I wanted to tell the story I was learning daily about race in America. But there were so many layers, so much anger, so much shame and sheer confusion, I often found myself remaining silent just when I most yearned to speak aloud. At times I would narrate tales to my closest friends, my sister, my niece, white people whom I knew would try to learn with me rather than argue with a perspective dramatically opposed to the one they, as whites, had been taught all their lives. Some of them worked closely with Black people, or their growing children were bringing home Black friends. Some of those who had been active in the civil rights movement, or worked actively against racism in other contexts, were learning the same lessons as I was about the doubleness of American reality, the literal madness of white denial about so much connected to race. At times I wrote, in essays and fiction and always in my journals, about some aspect of this new and central story which was so dramatically shifting my perspective. I talked with other mothers about how the enormous desire to protect our children is made more and more futile as our children grow out of the circle of possible protection. I could follow Khary to school when he was in the second grade, making certain he crossed at the green, or that no insane kidnapper snatched him along his vulnerable way. But I could hardly follow a twenty-year-old man to the video store, watching for teenagers with guns with one eye, racist cops with the other.

I spoke about some of these experiences to a white friend who, with a sudden rush of insight, said, "It's the common story of motherhood, but with this terrible added dimension." And she pushed our consciousness forward an inch or two.

I spoke to a Black friend who raised her eyebrows, then tolerantly but with real gentleness, smiled.

I am sitting in a large circle of friends who for nearly twenty years have together attended an annual Seder, the ritual meal and storytelling that celebrates the Jewish holiday of Passover, marking the liberation of the Jews from slavery in Egypt. Rachel, the hostess and leader of the Seder, grew up Protestant in New England, converted to Judaism in her thirties and went on to become a rabbi, so she knows something about belonging and something about being a stranger; something about the slow pace of real change. On this night, she begins with the traditional words: *Once we were slaves in Egypt, but now we are free.* Slavery is a "narrow place," she tells us, a way of being that constrains, holds a person back or down; a heavy burdensome place where choice, individuality, and safety are obliterated, where the only possibilities are to labor, to obey, and to endure. The opposite of slavery, of course, is freedom, and we are invited to tell personal stories from the past year which illustrate either state.

A young woman talks about her workshops on family violence with high school students, the enslavement of gender definitions still dominant in American life. A mother tells the story of her son who has just come out as a gay man, and she describes the narrow space of people's reactions to him, even her own struggles with disapproval until the invisibility of his life opened her eyes and expanded the space around her. Rachel, who is recently widowed, describes blinding grief over the year since her husband's death, then the slow widening of vision that begins to suggest possible recovery.

Soon our personal stories broaden — because that is the requirement of the ritual of Seder — into talk of more collective enslavements and liberations. This is the year of the Gulf War and the widespread approval by the American people of the bombing of Iraq; it is a year which has seen the continuation of the steady disintegration into poverty and fear of our own neighborhood streets.

As the ritual Seder plate is passed around and we dip our bitter herbs into the salt water meant to represent tears, I remember accompanying Rachel to a sermon she gave in a Westchester temple. I listened along with an audience of Jews as this blond-haired rabbi described the idea of the Stranger in Jewish law, a concept which, in the Seder, is symbolized by the welcoming of Elijah; he is the uninvited guest who comes to the opened door to share in the drinking of the wine and the telling of the liberation story. He is the wanderer whom we must wait and provide for, without whom our ritual of remembrance and redemption is incomplete, because there is always a stranger, always someone new or forgotten knocking at the door. At a certain point in the ritual storytelling which accompanies the eating of symbolic foods, a child is asked to go to the door to welcome Elijah, and all watch the cup of wine set for him in the middle of the table, wait for him to drink.

When I was a child, attending a traditional Seder among my grandmother's siblings in Brooklyn, the story was told in Hebrew with partial and occasional translations on the side for the awestruck and mystified children. But when Elijah approached our table, I always thought I saw the level of wine in the goblet decrease.

As Rachel spoke from the platform of that wealthy Westchester synagogue, I heard whispers behind me. *Some Jew,* a woman murmured nastily. *A shikse (non-Jewish woman) if I ever saw one.* And connected by years of friendship to Rachel, having learned through her to understand something of the best spirit of Judaism, I knew that in the world of religion I would always be the Stranger in a way.

I had never questioned my Jewishness which is as thick and real as the food smells, the language of Yiddish, the musical rhythms and psychological patterns I grew up surrounded by. But now I remembered another temple where recently, inspired by the strong cultural identification which had released the spirits of so many people I knew, I attended a Yom Kippur service. In that temple on the Day of Atonement, although I was moved by the symbolic meaning of the holiday (the relationship between atonement and cleansing, between forgiveness of others and forgiveness of the self), the emotional experience evident on the faces of others was elusive for me. I felt only that I wanted to go home, which meant four rooms in a building several blocks away.

I suppose it was because I found cultural belonging to be so attractive and yet eternally problematic that at Rachel's Seder, where I was surrounded by old friends, I wanted to tell some of the story of American Blackness I was learning to understand as Adam and Khary began to grow into men. Where better to tell this story of liberations, of broadening visions? But I was reticent, afraid too many would misunderstand. They would think it was only because of love for my children, but the reality is the children are the cause of a change in myself. The fortunate accident of loving a Black man and becoming a mother of Black children has enabled me to see the world more truthfully.

The sentence I have just written seems simple — a straightforward idea, uncomplicated words. But it has taken a long time to construct it so directly. A conversion, as Rachel might remind me, with its requirement for reassessment, study, and change, can take many years.

During that year's Passover, no one in my family speaks. I wait, hoping one of them will talk about being Black, about racism, but when I look around the room with their eyes and see that everyone is white, I realize they will not speak, and most likely no one else here will speak of racism escalating in our country because race is not often the first thing on white people's minds.

Spirited back to a much earlier Seder, I hear Adam's ten-year-old voice. We have reached the part of the narrative that describes the Jews in their escape to freedom coming to the Red Sea which is parted by God so Moses and the Israelites can pass over safely to the other side. When their Egyptian pursuers enter the space between the parting of the waters, the sea closes over them and all of them are drowned.

"What do they do with the people who are half Jewish and half Egyptian?" I hear Adam say, a look of anxiety knitting his dark brows.

I sit among friends at the Seder and listen to the story of slavery and freedom, about the long journey from one to the other through the wilderness of exile and doubt, and I am not able to retrieve into words the story of narrowness or renewed life I am beginning to comprehend. Its shape is still forming in my imagination. Embedded in contrary feelings and undigested realizations, I am nowhere near the end of the wilderness and often I feel it is not possible, nor even desirable, to speak.

Perhaps it is because a classroom, at its best, can be a safe place to express ignorance and uncertainty as well as knowledge; perhaps it is because age and preparation have enabled a teacher to know more and thus feel more confident than anyone else in the room; but also, teaching, like writing, creates a space outside ordinary space, and time outside ordinary time, so that for a finite number of hours, focus and concentration (with the hope of new insight) can become extraordinary as well. As difficult as I found it to express my experiences to friends and family, I was eager and excited as I began to change much of my teaching to reflect this new and central concern of my life.

For all the years I had taught fiction by African Americans — Zora Neale Hurston, James Baldwin, Paule Marshall, Toni Morrison, and others — I had counted on the emotional identification these works engendered in students of all backgrounds. Themes of voice and silence, of visibility and invisibility, of the recreation of self that can come with telling one's own story — all these motifs provoked students' thinking and writing as dramatically as they had my own. One of the most powerful insights was always about the expansion of moral and psychological vision that can occur when the writer shifts point of view. When John, James Baldwin's protagonist in *Go Tell It on the Mountain,* seeks to free himself from hatred of his brutal father, he has to learn his father's story. Baldwin presents that story with the father at the center, as John will have to see it, a story that looks beyond the facts of bitterness and abusiveness to their origins and development.[5] Similarly, in Toni Morrison's *The Bluest Eye,* just as readers are coming to hate Pauline, the mother who hates herself and rejects her child, or Cholly, the father who rapes, we are forced into their stories from their own points of view.[6] Simple hatred is no longer possible. Easy condemnation is complicated by empathy and understanding. The idea of history becomes inextricably interwoven with individual tragedy, a condition of escape from righteousness. Point of view, then, is not only an aspect of narrative and aesthetic technique, but has an important ethical dimension as well.

A shift in point of view was certainly what I was experiencing, and this connection emboldened me to begin to teach African American autobiography and what is now called "race studies," although most of my students were white and I was still in the process of learning myself.

Once again I recall the words of Chinua Achebe from his essay on truth and fiction: "Things are then not merely happening *before* us; they are happening, by the power and force of imaginative identification, *to* us. We not only see; we *suffer* alongside the hero and are branded by the same mark . . ."[7]

But how do you achieve this imaginative identification when there is no novelist organizing perspective, unlayering the stories that lie within and occurred before the stories we too simplistically call "our lives"?

Following my trip to the Richmond Museum, I had come to see the African American autobiographical tradition as a powerful example of the formal possibilities and thematic depths of a growing and changing genre. The writing for the course I planned would be autobiographical too, I decided, so that each person could appreciate the "autobiographical attitude" as a pursuit of consciousness through a thicket of false namings; a ritual of self-creation and discovery. We all spoke personally from the outset, offering our own stories as one foundation for critical discussion. I modeled this approach by identifying myself in the first class as the white mother of Black sons, and described this experience as one of the most defining of my life.

There were ten white students and one African American in the group, and the African American woman said immediately that she felt uncomfortable being the "only one" especially due to the nature of the curriculum. Having articulated her skepticism, however, she decided to remain.

I explained for the first of many times my intellectual reasons for choosing the curriculum: the literary and historical importance of Black autobiographical texts as an American tradition; and, central for me as a reader, writer, and teacher, the restored connection in this tradition between the often polarized personal story and story of history. Black American writers "create dangerously," a phrase used by Albert Camus to describe the work of artists who combine personal truth with political vision.[8]

There is an interview in which James Baldwin speaks about his idea of the witness, a concept that lies at the heart of his entire body of work: "If one substitutes the word witness for writer and eliminates all romanticism about literature . . . some things become clear . . . [A]ll I know now is what I am trying to be a witness to . . . [I]t is a question of trying to translate what you see, trying to move it from one place to another."[9]

A witness, in this sense, means partaking, achieving a measure of imaginative identification. I was finding language for my own experience, hoping I could adequately lead students toward awareness of their own.

During a discussion of Patricia J. Williams's autobiographical narrative, *The Alchemy of Race and Rights,* in which she explores her life as a Black woman law professor, a problem arose. We were discussing a passage in which Williams recounts the paradoxical experience of feeling invisible and horribly visible in an all-white community.[10] We had just completed five weeks of serious, often emotionally charged discussion about race, identity, and history. Still, one student questioned the centrality of "Blackness" in Williams's experience, asserting that we all feel this terrible visibility/invisibility burden at times, challenging her special identification of it with race. I reminded her of our discussions about the importance of listening to detail in stories different from our own, and confirmed that in my view race would have to be a notable center for Williams, whatever resonant universal echoes there might also be. Then there was silence. A silence that lasted for some minutes. And there we were, nine white people and one Black person, discussing the issue of visibility and invisibility, no one mentioning the fact that we were enacting exactly the situation Williams described.

I knew the Black student fairly well, and we trusted each other. But I felt it would be presumptuous of me to identify her into perhaps painful visibility by pointing out what she must surely be feeling. However, not to point it out was equally objectifying of her. She said nothing. No one else spoke. The subject was changed. After class, when she and I spoke privately, I explained that I didn't know if my speaking would have made matters better or worse. She said my speaking would have made matters neither better nor worse, that this had been but one example of the difficulties of being the only Black person in all white classes. She chose not to raise the issue again, although I offered to support her in any way she wished.[11]

I know now that teaching African American studies, which inevitably raises issues of race and racism in all our lives, is fraught with special problems for a white teacher who, even with the best intentions, will make mistakes, offend unwittingly, discover areas of surprising ignorance within ourselves, or simply be impotent to protect, as I was in this case. I strongly believe that white teachers can and should continue to teach African American history and literature. Since the 1970s, when I began to teach fiction by Black women writers to largely African American and Latina classes at the City College of New York, I have never questioned my ability to understand and empathize with African American writers and their characters. As with any other subject, it is a matter of learning context and responding to universal theme. Obviously, I did not live the life of Sethe, for example, an American slave escaped to freedom in Ohio in Toni Morrison's *Beloved,* any more than I lived the life of Jane Eyre, a Christian, working-class governess in nineteenth-century England. But my life has been structured by many of the same themes Morrison uses to structure her novel about Sethe and her sacrificed daughter, Beloved: the themes of lost and recovered memory, its dangers and salvations; of the intricate interior reflections of the experience of slavery and the human need for liberty; of the overlapping identities of motherhood and daughterhood.

But I think we have to be clear about our limits, how much there is to learn in terms of intellectual perspective and emotional sensitivity. We must approach this aspect of teaching with a great deal of humility, realizing that we have all sorts of prejudices and areas of ignorance about everything from the cultural connotations of seemingly neutral language — (I only recently realized that the word *denigrate* means to "blacken and therefore defame") — to blindness to African American perspectives in our dominant cultural life. (Think, for example, of an African American watching a commercial on television that invited us to "come down to colonial Williamsburg, where everything is the same now as it was then." I watched it with Adam and experienced the now-familiar jolt of altered perspective when he responded, "No thanks, I think I'll pass on that one." Some months later, when certain groups organizing that theme park decided to include a slave market, dramatizing a slave auction with Black actors playing the slaves of colonial Williamsburg, there was great controversy. For how could a slave market be dramatized without trivializing the awful history? Would the "slaves" be paraded naked before the buyers who explored their bodies as they might animals' bodies for quality of teeth and muscle, strongness of limbs? Yet, how could the slave market be erased if accuracy were to be served? As soon as African American history is included into written or visual texts of American history, our troubled past is revealed. Simple additions of new material will not solve the problem, and substantive revisions bring a deeper sense of truth to any story. Previous structures of meaning will topple from the new insights and, as with a conceptual revision of any manuscript, the story may have to be rewritten from the beginning to the end.)

During the closing weeks of the semester of my class, a white student who had been upset about the curriculum confronted me. He could not accept African American autobiography being used as a paradigm for the intellectual reasons I offered, but insisted I was "favoring" this tradition for my own personal reasons. Questioning the integrity of autobiographical motivation in teaching, he accused me of intellectual dishonesty and the language he used, unsurprisingly, was the language of current fashion: I was imposing a "politically correct" curriculum on him and silencing his views. He felt, as many white male students do, I find, deeply attracted to Black cultural life, especially some of its more "macho" aspects. Yet he felt both exiled from it and defensive about being a white male as the social constructions of race and gender are increasingly challenged.

In this course (called "Autobiography and Writing the Self") African American autobiography was presented as the model of a genre, as opposed to an explicitly signed study — "African American Literature," or "Slavery in the United States." When African American writing was offered as a standard of universality, this student became uncomfortable, feeling left out, highly visible and invisible, feeling, in other words, the daily experience of so many African American students in largely white classes reading all-white texts. He was in a kind of shock at having the story line altered, the plot thickened by a sudden shift in point of view.

As I continued my work of revising the course, trying to imagine ways of discussing race in the classroom without sacrificing individual stories, yet also without exchanging an intellectual search for reductive and unreflective personal testimony, the issue of race and racism came up again in a fiction writing class.

This time the (only) African American student read a portion of a memoir about having a white mother but seeing herself as a Black woman. Several of the white students challenged her, not on the basis of her writing but questioning her identification as Black. Familiar themes and conflicts ensued. The African American woman tried to be responsive, but eventually became angry and resistant, saying no one else was challenged on basic assumptions of who they were. One white student insisted she was blind to color differences, did not "see" race, suggesting that the Black woman was purposely and unnecessarily defining herself as different. When the Black woman responded angrily to this, three white students stated they felt "silenced" by her, and in general by (even single) Black students in many of their classes. Another student agreed that she was sick of all the "P. C." constraints on discussions about race. There were several white students who took a very different view, tried to talk about how ignorant most whites are about matters of race and African American life, that perhaps it would be appropriate to listen to the Black student's story more respectfully and critique it on its own terms. These students, unsurprisingly, were the most sophisticated about African American studies, had taken courses, read and thought seriously about race.

And I began wondering, as I said to my fiction writing class, where the burning issues of one's time must come into the discussions as students write their visions and their lives; I began wondering about what this new word, "P. C.," has come to mean. In contemptuously calling something P. C. are we denying the idea that racial insults, however unintentioned, cause pain? That insensitivity to the lives of others, failures of imaginative identification, should be struggled against?

I have taught a course in freshmen writing for many years called "Voice and Silence" in which I work to facilitate individual voice in young students, but also introduce them to the idea that silence and silencing have a political and social history as well as a place in their individual psyches, and that this wider history enlightens and gives contextual meaning to their own experiences. In reading Tillie Olsen's *Silences,* which traces constrictions on writers because of class and gender[12], or Alice Walker's "In Search of Our Mothers' Gardens,"[13] which identifies a legacy of Black maternal voices not generally heard, these young people coming of age in the 1990s see themselves.

But what do white students and other white people mean when they talk about being silenced? Is it wrong to feel silenced, if being silenced is taken to mean feeling humbled by all one does not yet understand, including the scope of one's own prejudice? Is this "feeling silenced" at times simply a recognition that without careful thinking and concerted self-examination, any white person is likely to have a harder time than a person of color fully understanding how our society is racialized in nearly every way?

Would it not be true, then, that the more one is a white person of good faith and antiracist values, the more uncomfortable, unwilling to thoughtlessly offend, and therefore sometimes "silenced" one might feel in discussions about race with other Americans who are of African descent? How could this not be so?

I think again of Baldwin's witness, of partaking, being part of the story; of Achebe's imaginative identification suggesting the possibility of shared feeling among very different people. But how can either be achieved without the patience to listen to the multitude of details making up stories not your own? It is not that we cannot understand each other, but that we presume that understanding too quickly, close the unfamiliar story down with our own intrusive narrating, have no patience or endurance for the difficult times of exile — that wilderness which can often feel lonely and unsafe.

All this time I am hoping and planning that some day I will be able to put down on paper this story of mixed bloods and joined cultural heritages, a story more layered and new than either Douglas or I imagined when I told him in the winter of 1969 that I was pregnant with our first child. But even now there are threads not taken up which must be woven into the fabric. For I am not simply raising Black *children,* but

Black sons, and in a world where life is surely as "gendered" as it is "raced," a society in which race and sexuality have always been murderously intertwined, the demand for identifying imaginatively will be great indeed.

II

One of the most defining moments in history when he was coming of age, Douglas has told us many times, was the killing of Emmitt Till, a fourteen-year-old boy from Chicago who, while visiting his family in Mississippi, "made some remarks" (according to the *New York Times* of September 1955 when the incident occurred) and "wolf whistled" at a white woman. His disfigured body, tortured and maimed beyond easy identification, was found in the Tallahatchie River after a three-day search. "He was about the same age as I was at the time — and we hadn't heard of such a bad lynching in a long time," Douglas says in a typically understated tone. But he brings his palms down silently and slowly until they are flat on the table, and I hear a profound quietness which, at rare times, is a precursor of tears.

When I ask Khary about his reaction to this piece of history, he says: "For my generation, Emmitt Till has become Yusef Hawkins [the young man who was killed in Bensonhurst, Brooklyn], Michael Griffith [murdered in Howard Beach, Queens], Philip Pennel [shot in the back in Teaneck, New Jersey], Michael Stewart [beaten to death for writing graffiti on the Number One train in Manhattan]. As with lynchings," — Khary's arms are folded across the table in front of him much as his father's might be — "each one represents many anonymous deaths just like them. And at least one of them — Yusef Hawkins — was murdered because it was thought he was involved with a white woman. It's still a constant theme in some places. My friends from the South tell me that in many places you still don't talk publicly to white girls."

As always in these discussions, I feel masked and disguised, trapped by a skin I cannot change, or as if my skin is separate from *me*. I look at him and talk to him from behind this foreign thing — my skin (no longer perfect and simple protection for tissue, flesh, and bone, it is something to be overcome). I want to get out of it so I can be sure he sees *me,* yet I know I am in it. It *is* me. I try to imagine myself a child of three, or four, or five, having these feelings, looking at his skin, wondering about the meanings lodged there.

"But the fear of violence in a place like New York," Khary is saying in an urgent tone, "is mostly of the police. When you see some white guys maybe getting a fine when they jump a turnstile — you think if I did that I might get shot. And beyond the police, there is a lot of implied, potential violence between white and Black men. Young white guys on the street are afraid of Black men, especially if we are in groups. When kids or women seem afraid of me, I feel bad. I think, can't you see I'm not going to hurt you? But with white men, when they're scared, I don't feel bad about it."

I sit across the table from my son as he reveals these feelings about fearing and being feared. I want to protect him from the spiritual assault of being made to feel threatening, always threatening. Yet, I am coming to see that he and Adam must learn to "handle themselves" — that perfectly self-splitting/self-possessing phrase — if they are to be safe and thus relatively free.

I wish for clear, simple statements: this is about being a man or a woman; this is about being Black or about being white; this is how the question of violence weaves into wider patterns like a brightly colored, easily visualized thread. I remember him as a small boy who cried about the violence in football, a game he loved to play, and about the violence in the world at large. I remember Adam, refusing to watch movies and television films about slavery if there was a scene of lynching. And Khary, learning in high school the terrible, long history of lynching in an independent study course. Recently, I read through one of his books on the grim and horrifying statistics, the common practice of cutting off then selling Black body parts after a lynching was complete, of beginning or ending a lynching with castration. He had underlined all the most gruesome details, all the signs of what, in other situations, Americans would refer to as genocide or holocaust. I am silent before the complexity of

overlapping categories facing me in the face of my son, in my own face —
whiteness, Blackness, man, woman, boy, girl.

I try to imagine the change from a typically childish fear of violence,
to an assessment of violence, accepting its prevalence, learning how to
gauge, manage, prepare for it. At some point in all sorrows, in any
compromise with futile desire, you begin to accept reality rather than
cling to a doomed wish that things were different from what they are. It's
the only way to keep going, to keep on keeping on.

This past winter in a small town in North Carolina, a twenty-one-year-
old Black man was murdered by a white man, the estranged husband of a
white woman who was involved with the Black man. Before he shot him,
the white man accused the Black man of raping his wife. But this was not
true, and the white woman, in order to help ward off threatened violence
from all sides, went on local television to say so. The white man was
arrested and taken to jail in another town for his own protection. The
young Black man's mother is the wife of one of Douglas's cousins, her
son Khary's and Adam's second cousin, murdered for being with a white
woman. She told us she was sometimes afraid she was going to take a
gun to her own head, the only way she could imagine to end her despair
for the loss of her child.

I think about the title of a collection of essays by Black women writers,
*All the Women Are White, All the Blacks Are Men, But Some of Us Are
Brave*,[14] the way that title critiques our categories, forces upon us all the
confusion felt by Black women made invisible by white and male dis-
course, recognizes all in one phrase that courage is the only resolution to
such monumental distortion. Am I a woman, thinking about male violence as I remember this recent family tragedy with my son? Am I a white
person facing him across the table, my heart sinking in shame?

I hear Adam's child voice; he is about ten years old and I am trying to
persuade him to walk away from fights with other boys in school: "He
called me a nigger, Mom. You want me not to hit him back?"

The low tones of Billie Holiday's voice, a voice that goes so low as to
verge on silence itself, a grief-stricken near paralysis of voice which wills
itself one more time into music and words: *Black bodies swinging in the*

southern breeze / Strange fruit hanging from the poplar trees. A history too recent and bloody to be forgotten, yet for many of us, unknown.

There is no simple stance for a mother of Black sons, no easy lesson to impart. Violence and race and sex form a disorderly pattern made invisible by the same cultural denial that obscures slavery itself. In a recent study about white women's attitudes toward race, a young white woman says: "[We learned in school] that there were parts of the country where things aren't so rosy. The south, that had slavery, and the thing that happened there all the time was that Black men wanted to rape white women."[15] There was no single moment when she learned this cruelly inverted truth, no single deception which turned the reality — of millions of Black women raped by white men within a system of brutality institutionalized over centuries — upside down. It is part of the way we lose knowledge in long-held, socially supported lies.

This particular lie affects Black boys not only in their sense of history, but in their bodies. The already difficult-to-negotiate terrain of male sexuality is entangled even further by the double bind: you are a sexual trophy and a certain rapist.

("I know white women are caught up with the idea that I want to rape them," Khary told me once; "or else, like a lot of white women in my school, they will *only* go out with Black guys.")

I think of the Black bodies which are the closest bodies to me in the world, their wonderful ordinariness, their ordinary wonder, and then — as if a merciless spotlight has changed a softening tone to a blinding, ugly white — I imagine Black bodies made to seem mysterious, threatening, holders of nightmares and dreams.

In Toni Morrison's *Beloved,* the self-named preacher, Baby Suggs, teaches a sermon in the forest that turns the Christian hatred of the body upside down.

" . . . we flesh;" she says. "[F]lesh that weeps, laughs; flesh that dances on bare feet in grass. Love it. Love it hard. Yonder they do not love your flesh. They despise it. They don't love your eyes; they'd just as soon pick em out. No more do they love the skin on your back. Yonder they flay it. And O my people they do not love your hands. Those they only use, tie, bind, chop off and leave empty. Love your hands! Love them. Raise them up and kiss them. Touch others with them, pat them together, stroke them on your face 'cause they don't love that either. *You* got to love it, *you!* And no, they ain't in love with your mouth. Yonder, out there, they will see it broken and break it again. What you say out of it they will not heed. What you scream from it they do not hear. What you put into it to nourish your body they will snatch away and give you leavins instead. No, they don't love your mouth. *You* got to love it. This is flesh I'm talking about here. Flesh that needs to be loved."[16]

In Frederick Douglass's narrative of liberation and escape from slavery, there is a crucial moment in which he revives within himself a "sense of manhood." He has been given over to a "slave breaker" named Covey, a man famous for his success in bringing rebellious male slaves to submission through a methodical use of the whip accompanied by brutal kickings and regular beatings. At this turning point in the narrative and his life, Douglass tells us: "You have seen how a man was made into a slave; you shall see how a slave was made a man." He goes on to describe his slow crawling, then standing, then fighting his way out of Covey's physical and psychological domination, the difficult process of rebellion toward ultimate resolve: "I seized him with both hands by his collar and brought him by a sudden snatch to the ground." After the battle, in which Douglass triumphs, he explains: "He can only understand the deep satisfaction which I experienced, who has himself repelled by force the bloody arm of slavery. I felt as I have never felt before. It was a glorious resurrection, from the tomb of slavery to the heaven of freedom. My long-crushed spirit rose, cowardice departed, bold defiance took its place; and now I resolved that, however long I might remain a slave in form, the day had passed forever when I could be a slave in fact. I did not hesitate to let it be known of me, that the white man who expected to succeed in whipping, must also succeed in killing me."[17]

The body, brutalized and humiliated, stands up and its voice says — I will take no more. The place of enslavement and degradation is the flesh, and it is the flesh which must be the location of liberation as well. But I am also reading these pages as a mother of sons emerging into manhood in a city, a nation, and a world where violence threatens their flesh in a hundred ways, where I don't want their bodies to become instruments of violence threatening other bodies. I recall Frederick Douglass, long after this moment, speaking and writing about violence against the human spirit, against human flesh. And I am struck with admiration for his willingness, like that of so many other narrators of the experience of American slavery, including the fictional narrative of Toni Morrison, to tell the long version of the story, including the broken parts, not to leave the damage unclaimed. It is important to remember the damage. Because otherwise you pretend the narrow place of enslavement is not so bad after all. We can all cross the wilderness quickly, forget the forty years of wandering and concentrate only on the epiphany, as if it came out of nothing, suddenly, gracefully there. As they used to tell us children were born, erasing the pain, the agony of birthing: *and suddenly she was there.* Then pretending birth itself was the end of the story, the glorious moment overshadowing and distorting the story of motherhood, that long haul.

I feel the pride in Douglass' story of the turning point moment in his liberation. I feel at the heart of Baby Suggs' sermon the human need to be loved. Unloved, any/body who finds a way to survive must construct an imaginative pride, and I wonder if pride must always include hardness, must harden against attack, must protect with a wary defense against pain.

Perhaps this particular search came about in part *because* my sons were adolescents, beginning to map the ground of their own manhood. Between self-expression and discipline; between the raw and passionate heart and what George Eliot called "the self that self restrains"; between independence, that salient male virtue, and the dependent connections I cherish as the binding heart of love: perhaps more than ever before I wanted to imagine some balance as a lifelong vision for us all.

This is no easy trick for a mother of sons. As they moved from childhood, when feelings were raw and pure, into adolescence, I watched my sons pursue distance and armor as defense, while the girls I knew sought solace in confession to each other, their mothers, their aunts — a circle of women they would replicate throughout their lives. I often found myself wishing for more solid armor in the girls, more honest confession in the boys, two aspects of courage as gender-divided in our society as the trucks and dolls of their infant playrooms.

"You shall be a child of the mother," Robin Morgan wrote around the time of my children's births in a poem I memorized and loved; "and your face shall not be turned from me."[18] But their faces do turn, pulled in various directions by the world around them, and just when you long to take them in your arms, you are reminded by a turned back, an anger, or a sorrow you really don't understand, that maternal advice misplaced or misspoken can prolong the period before they turn back to assess what they have left behind. A new kind of silence enters your home, a new kind of reticence and fear.

Often I question Douglas closely, asking for his memories and interpretations as a man, as a Black man. His thoughts are reliable borders encouraging me to make my undocumented way.

"All my feelings about not appearing vulnerable come from deep inside me," he once explained. "One of my clearest childhood memories is of being treated like a young adult, even when I was five or six, and I realize, as I reflect on it, that this was common in Black families at the time. I hardly recall any instance of my father expressing physical affection to me. Black families have to turn their sons into men quickly, because they have to shoulder so much responsibility and withstand so many aspects of racism. This goes all the way back to slavery."

"Be what you want — white or black. Choose," says Lestory, a Black man and former slave, to his son of a white mother in Toni Morrison's *Jazz*. "But if you choose black, you got to act black, meaning draw your manhood up — quicklike, and don't bring me no whiteboy sass."[19]

"There's a kind of ideology of what it means to be strong," Douglas tells me. "Don't be overly emotional, don't cry, make the best of things, and go on."

I remember Khary, then about five years old, sitting on his grandmother's lap as she moved back and forth in a rocking chair. Suddenly she said, with tears in her eyes, "I never held my own boys in my lap when they were this big. I have never held a boy whose legs were long enough to reach the ground."

And Baldwin's words in *Notes Of A Native Son:* "And when the children were hungry and sullen and distrustful and one watched them, daily, growing wilder, and further away, and running headlong into danger, it was the Lord who knew what the charged heart endured as the strap was laid to the backside; the Lord alone who knew what one *would* have said if one had had, like the Lord, the gift of the living word. It was the Lord who knew of the impossibility every parent in that room faced: how to prepare the child for the day when the child would be despised and how to *create* in the child — by what means? — a stronger antidote to this poison than one had found for oneself."[20]

Douglas did hold his children, will still shower his grown sons with kisses as he murmurs, I love you, Sugar. But patterns change unevenly in relation to the uneven demands of the world. "Pride," says Douglas, "is partly about not seeming vulnerable. It is about being able to take whatever they throw at you. A friend of mine put it this way: never let them see you sweat."

During my sons' adolescence, when they sometimes became fierce or inaccessible, I was afraid I'd be helpless to combat the powerful male ideals I felt sure I'd lose them to. As a result, I argued too often for simple vulnerability, unlimited self-revelation, failing to acknowledge how often I myself found it hard to speak, even to write the autobiography I spent so much of my time encouraging students to do. (Even now, I stop in midstream of this writing, to wash dishes, make a call, read a book, go out to buy fish for dinner.)

Then for a time, I went over to the other side, practicing self-control in nearly every aspect of my life, playing the part of the strong, self-contained woman until I became that woman too. I grew comfortable with the way she acted and spoke, with what she could hide. I was happier, felt stronger that way.

"If you can't be free be a mystery," a friend told me once, quoting from a poem by Rita Dove.[21] My friend is a Black man whose poetry and music open up spaces frightening and dangerous to expose, yet who seems, himself, to have mastered the art of self-containment. He tells only what he wants to tell, keeps his wits about him. A proud man. Under control. *If you can't be free be a mystery.* Yes, I would think. I want to be like that, and be clear and safe forever.

Around this time, the summer of 1992, Khary needs arthroscopic surgery, a minor operation on the knee. Although I try to discuss any fears he might have about the operation, Khary is a young man of eighteen, and even sensitive young men do not easily confess fears to their mothers, or even, perhaps, to themselves. "There is nothing to worry about," he insists. "It's a minor operation; everything is under control." His annoyance with my questions silences me quickly, and I force myself to believe in the casualness of his anticipation as much as he does himself.

After a ten-minute procedure performed by a famous white surgeon, Douglas and I, waiting anxiously in the hallway, are told Khary will be out of anesthesia in minutes and we can see him them. We stand outside the recovery room while minutes become an hour, and still there is no word. Maternal terrors fill my head, and I begin desperately asking the nurses what is going on. I am told he is still not out of surgery, that he is "having trouble" coming out of the anesthesia. In a panic, I nevertheless go into action, calling the famous doctor, who by now is back in his office, shouting and threatening (encouraged by the nurses who are obviously furious that they do not know any more than we do, and who are nearly all Black). The doctor is back within minutes, genuinely worried and also, no doubt, afraid of suit. After going back in to see Khary, he emerges to tell us the following story.

Khary has repeatedly come out of the anesthesia violently, thrashing and flailing about. With most young people Khary's age, the doctor tells us, there would be no problem; the doctors and nurses would gently but firmly hold him down. Our son, however, is "so large and powerful," they are worried that he might injure himself or the medical personnel, and therefore they have to keep sending him back under rather than simply restraining him with their hands.

This happens to be the summer following the acquittal of the police officers in the beating of Rodney King. The repeated descriptions of my eighteen-year-old son, who admittedly is six feet tall and athletic but no body builder, as "enormous and powerful" resonates with descriptions of Rodney King as an "inhumanly powerful animal" and back to the nurse in the delivery room calling my crying, six-pound baby a "militant Black Panther."

We insist upon seeing him immediately and are suddenly told we can go into the recovery room where we can see for ourselves that "nothing is wrong."

He is obviously agitated, floating in and out of consciousness, turning over onto his stomach and covering his head with his arms, a movement which threatens to dislodge the IV. Seeing he is afraid, not angry or violent, Douglas and I lean over him, whispering gently, stroking his head and shoulders, and soon he begins to calm down. As soon as he does, the doctors begin to stroke his head too, to whisper gently, *calm down, it's all right*. And I am convinced that in the operating room, they were too rough, holding him down in a way that could only have increased his fear. I watch them closely as they lean over him now, their gentle words and gestures ringing slightly false, as if they are copying our gestures and words, and I would swear they are ashamed; that they see what I have seen — that they handled the situation badly, with fear instead of tenderness.

Later, when he is in his own bed, drowsy and relaxed, I ask Khary again about his thoughts before the operation. He tells me he remembered movies he has seen about patients dying or disappearing after some minor operation, about the blind trust we put in strangers just because they are doctors. He thought about all this as he watched the anesthesiologist inject the chemicals into his IV.

Now it is clear that he was frightened when he went under and frightened when he began to wake up. Being a boy, in some ways already a man, he had learned to manage fear with stolid denial, a conscious bravery which contains anxiety but which can also become fragile when consciousness is suspended for a time. Being Black, white doctors were no symbol of security and superior knowledge for him. Rather, their skins must have triggered many stories of terror, their faces looming over him as he tried to resist sinking into unconsciousness and loss of control.

After about an hour of lying in his own bed, he falls asleep again, turning onto his stomach as always, and I notice large bruises on his shoulders and neck.

Raising boys, teaching and learning from young men, I sometimes feel a physical sensation of muteness from the complexity of overlapping patterns, centuries old, that we, their feminist mothers, are asking them to unravel and redesign.

A white, male, heterosexual, feminist student, someone I greatly admire, has immersed himself in the study of male violence for several years. Battering, rape, war: he has studied them all. His papers are so full of condemnations of masculinity that I finally ask him to come to my office where I try to talk to him about the good things about being a man. As we talk through the cool, darkening afternoon, I find myself using Adam's words as I speak to him about providing; about enduring pain, and moving directly toward a goal; about paternal and fraternal loyalty or protection; the ability to remain self-confident despite failure and fear; the magnetism of a man with his eyes on the world: traditional masculine virtues many women also want to claim.

Long an admirer and reader of Black women writers, Khary takes a college course in that rich American literary tradition. After six or seven novels in which male characters are ruthless, dominating, and violent, at best desperate and enraged, he says to his professor and his class: "I see it's very important to write these stories, because they're true. I'm not suggesting changes in these novels, because I've heard Black women say this is really what their lives are like. But aren't there some other novels with other images? Are there no fathers or brothers, not an uncle or a cousin, who was kind and supportive, who could be put into the stories of our lives?"

I thought I heard a slight break in his voice when he told me this story over the phone one night. I remembered the particular shade of pain that seemed to come across his face like fog when he watched the conviction of Mike Tyson, heard the Nicole Simpson tapes confirming O.J.'s history of abuse.

Yet, at the conclusion of O.J. Simpson's trial, after the jury acquitted him, race and gender became dangerously confused for many white Americans. I heard many white women insist on Simpson's guilt *because* he had battered his wife, as if no other evidence had been central to the year-long trial. The image of a Black man, possibly wrongly accused, certainly victim of some lying on the part of the police, held no resonance for most whites as it did for most of the Black people I knew. As the mostly Black jury was patronized and insulted, their very words about their reasons for their verdict erased by most white commentators and reporters, the history of racism and American criminal justice was made to seem parenthetical, at best a diversion from the "objective" verdict that might have been rendered by a predominantly white jury. During this time, the intellectual and emotional convolutions of American race and gender attitudes were painfully manifest.

After Nicole Simpson's taped plea for help was released, there was increased public recognition for a while about family violence. From the television screen, testimony of battered women from all backgrounds and classes filled our living room night after night, faces darkened and voices altered for anonymity, but their words eerily the same: *Why did he hit me? Oh, I didn't cook the pasta long enough, or I cooked it too long, or I didn't vacuum well enough, or I made too much noise with the vacuum while he was trying to nap or watch the game.*

Men envisioning women in their lives as servicers, providers of absolute love and domestic comfort; an infant's version of a perfect mother who herself could never have existed in such inhuman form.

One day I am riding the subway uptown when a huge group of high school students gets on. The rest of us are shoved into each other, pushed against the seats while we listen to the boys taunt each other across the car, the girls giggling and rolling their eyes. Two voices take over, escalating the anger until all the passengers over a certain age, white and Black, Asian and Latino, women and men, are looking at each other with anxiety, shaking our heads and raising our eyebrows in disapproval and fear. (Perhaps, one of these volatile teenagers is carrying a gun and once again "normal" male conflict which in previous times might have resulted in a fist fight will result, instead, in death.) One of the boys is moving toward the door, about to get off the train, and when he is standing on the platform, safely behind closing doors, he shouts, "Your mother is a whore." The doors close, and we can see him laughing and pointing, having gotten away with casting this ultimate insult. The boy who remains in the car punches the door several times, then raises his chin into the air, clenches his teeth. None of us looks at him for long; we turn our backs if we can in the small space, condemning and afraid.

A narrow place, masculinity thus defined. The palms raised in prayer to the worshipped mother are only the undersides of the fists clenched to strike each other and the women in their lives. Like many others, living in fear of the violence of men, I have welcomed and been changed by the feminist analysis of masculinity in its most destructive aspects.

But right now I am thinking of the confusion and despair in the faces of many young men I have known when the subject of male violence comes up. I recall the words of bell hooks: "[W]e talk about the way white people who shift locations . . . begin to see the world differently. Understanding the way racism works, [they can see] the way in which whiteness acts to terrorize without seeing [themselves] as bad, or all white people as bad, and all black people as good."[22]

She calls this process "crossing over." And I see we have to help the boys and young men cross over, strong enough to see how maleness can act to terrorize, without drowning in the self-deprecating belief that all men are bad, all women good. But how can we do this without seeing their stories within ourselves?

Then I have an experience at school which illuminates in my own life their complicated ambivalence toward vulnerability. It is one of those experiences accompanied by a confusion so powerful I know it is a signal of depth. It is as if I am caught in one of those "sneaker waves" I learned about once on the Pacific coast. They move in several directions at once, seemingly restricted to the foamy surface of the ocean but actually signifying currents so deep and contrary they can suck you down without warning, twisting and spinning menacingly all the way down to the ocean floor.

I am serving on a search committee at school, looking for a professor of African American history. It is an "affirmative action" search, which among other standards means that like many largely white institutions, we are trying to diversify our faculty and our student body. I am strongly committed to this work, serving on many search committees, because I am convinced by experiences like the ones described before that without African American and Latino faculty and students, multicultural curriculum and thus intellectual truth becomes a fraud.

One of the finalists is a woman of middle age, perhaps forty or forty-one years old. I will call her Suzanne. She has an impressive resume, including a privileged education, world travel, honors, and degrees. Yet, she seems held back professionally, somehow trapped. Her work, our resident historians worry, is characterized by the same curious inhibition or restraint as her life seems to be.

Her face is youthful, but beneath her chin and in the slight tightness of her jaw you can see a sign of age. Her eyes are almond-shaped and black, her skin a rich wet-earth brown. Her black hair is parted in the middle and a thick braid crowns her head meeting itself at the base of her neck. The style is completely natural, not set in a "natural" or stylized fashion, just thick, soft clouds of kinky hair pulled back neatly and woven into a crown. Her clothes are soft too, but under the loose silk jacket is an ordinary white T-shirt, lightly frayed at the neck. On the first day of the interviews, she wears high heeled shoes and shimmering stockings. On the second day, she wears old, soft flats, adding another old-fashioned aspect to her dress and style. Yet nothing seems to be done for style; it is all unstudied, all the looseness to comfort and contain rather than to display.

She pauses for long moments before she answers questions, speaks low, and if someone disagrees with her she neither presses her point nor changes her mind; she remains silent. The only Black person on our committee, G., tells us he believes she is scared. Why should she be scared, someone else wonders, with all those honors and degrees?

She speaks of Ku Klux Klan rallies in the town where she teaches, refers obliquely to a poor childhood, talks of how much she would like to move to New York even though ours is a small and not widely known college; even though, like most newcomers, she is afraid of the city. Her intelligence and passion for her work are unmistakable, but key members of the committee keep noticing that restraint. The word *reticent* comes up again. Perhaps even narrow.

After the first day, I find myself becoming restrained with her, almost shy. I am aware of a confusing ambivalence toward her which has nothing to do with her academic work or credentials. Something about her unnerves me. *That is the word: unnerve. She makes me feel I want to hide, that I have lost my nerve.* I feel intimidated, yet I can see she is doing nothing intimidating. Although she speaks articulately about American history and the way she would teach it, she refrains from any personal revelation, any critique of academia in general or the particular universities where she has taught. When she is asked a question she doesn't want to answer, she withdraws into that unnerving silence and ever so slightly tilts, then nods her head, as if she is listening intently to the question but is too overwhelmed by her thoughts to respond.

I overhear her speaking with the student committee and she is warmly engaged with them, sounding confident in her own purposes and attitudes about teaching, far more confident than she did with us.

That evening we invite her to attend a poetry reading by one of the faculty whose work I especially admire. Yet, fatigued and eager to go home, I wait anxiously for the end, then watch from a distance as she talks to others, sips wine. Suddenly, all I can think about is wanting to be in my own room, far away from everyone in the world.

Something about her vulnerability — the clothes, the braids, the fear.

She makes me think of my need to be alone, to live in my private thoughts, to write without thought of reader or critic. She makes me think about my fear of rejection, that common writer's fault of being too fragile to withstand all the criticism, of being too weak to take it, of not measuring up — and that phrase sticks in my mind: not measuring up.

She makes me think of my childhood insomnia. Frightened by a mixture of interior chaos and emptiness, I would try to maintain a perfectly directed consciousness and thus avoid sleep which at those times felt like death to me. This is the childhood memory that comes back to me as I stand on the other side of the room from her and remember how her head shook in confirmation as the poet read about being an interpreter for welfare mothers, reciting their words in English, then Spanish, translating the anguish and the pain.

She has asked me to put her in a cab before I leave, as she is afraid of the nighttime streets, and I rush up to her now, hurrying her to leave. Suddenly annoyed and dignified, she says coldly, "May I just finish my wine?" And there is no doubt at all that in this passing moment of her anger, I sense her strength and feel relief.

On the way home I think about all my strong women friends, of how all of us are subject to regular losses of confidence, unable, despite many achievements, to dissipate a bottom layer of intense self-doubt. Why does she seem so fragile, this woman who has achieved so much? Beaten down, G. said of her when we talked privately. This woman has been beaten down.

In terms of objective standards, the key members of the committee decide, we cannot hire her. We need leaders on this faculty. If she were stronger, more brave . . .

Several nights later, I have this dream: I am walking after an elegant, tall woman who is turning around every so often to talk to me over her shoulder. As she does so, I feel small, tolerated, and exposed, like a young child on one of those leashes people attach to toddlers as if they were dogs. The tall woman is self-confident, secure; *she has her nerve.* She wears her clothes well, her makeup is on right, she is graceful, makes the most of her beauty. She is looking down on me and I am not measuring up.

I wake up thinking about Suzanne's braids, the frayed neckline of her T-shirt beneath the silk jacket.

Covered wounds, layers of armor, scabs of coldness protecting against repeated pain. Chips on the shoulder of warning, at least a temporary respite of disconnection. A paralysis worth the price. Billie Holiday's sorrowful blues: *No one to see, I'm free as the breeze.* A certain kind of pride.

But some of us don't always measure up. Too beaten down, our need for admiration and love too enormous, perhaps we are eaten up by our own rage and grief, and we show up for interviews with old T-shirts visible beneath our new jackets, halting speech as we swallow the silences along with the words in our mouths, the angry words and the begging words, and the confusion too close to the surface: I am afraid of you. You will hurt me again. You will kill me again.

I remember the relief of finding armor that — no matter how clumsy or obvious it might have seemed to others — enabled me to move around. And I thought about how Suzanne's reticence and restraint must have been intensified by our whiteness, reflecting the whiteness of the universities in which she has studied and worked. If most of us had been Black, would she have seemed different, stronger, more free? We encounter the world in our bodies, and through our bodies' most exquisitely sensitive sense, our skins, we take the world into ourselves. We have made and remade a world where nearly every experience is shaded and shaped by the color of those bodies, the tones of those skins. It may take most of a lifetime to achieve the courage of vulnerability while remaining resiliant and strong, to possess the self-confidence and pride evident in the old blues lyrics: "If you see me comin', better open up your door / I ain't no stranger. I been here before."[23] To feel the safety and confidence, the entitlement, of those who know they belong.

I am in Provincetown, Massachusetts, attending a concert by Odetta, the great African American folk singer. After many songs combining jazz rhythms, folk, and blues, she has created a musical intimacy with the audience, chorused by commentary about politics, the disintegration of American cities, the horror of war and stories of her own life. When she comes to her final song, "Amazing Grace," she teaches us the lyrics, changing "a wretch like me" to "a soul like me." "No wretches here," she says. Finally, after we have sung it along with her three times and are in the middle of the fourth round, she bows and leaves the stage. We are still singing. The concert is over and she is gone; nevertheless, hundreds of us sitting in the crowded auditorium finish our song. As we sing without a leader, no one on the stage, a completely unusual feeling takes over. There is no performer. It is us. We are the singers. The words are ours.

Now, we begin to applaud until she returns, and then we all stand, shouting and clapping. She starts to sing again, *amazing grace,* and bows as we sing with her, throws us kisses, is crying herself, her soft purple gown undulating around her torso and knees. She leaves the stage again. This time we are standing while singing, and we continue, no leader to focus our emotions upon. It is our emotion, our voices, our amazing grace. *I once was lost but now I'm found,* we sing, echoing a story she told about herself as a child, a little Black girl who had come to loathe herself. We must overcome that, she said with stern conviction. We stand until we are finished with the verse and then we begin again, *I once was lost but now I'm found, was blind but now I see,* singing more softly now as people begin to leave the auditorium. As I think about mothering sons into manhood, about trying to imagine the inner life of a young Black man, about trying to overcome what can never be fully overcome, and although for long moments my voice will not make sound, I am able to sing some of the words.

Last year, as always, Rachel called us to the Seder. This time only Douglas and I are there from our family, Adam and Khary in different cities unable to come home. Douglas is the only Black person in the room. *Once we were slaves in Egypt,* Rachel tell us, *and now we are free.* And then the question, once again: what is slavery? We are invited to describe that narrow place.

People of serious moral consciousness, some of them our oldest friends, begin to talk about the Jews in Russia, the Muslims in Bosnia, the war in Somalia, the Kurds in Iraq and, because these are people who are committed to fairness and against domination and war, about the suffering of the Palestinian people on the West Bank.

When it is Douglas's turn, I can see he has decided to speak out once again, to resist the combination of exhaustion and anger which often makes Black people choose silence instead of yet another instructional speech to an all-white group. He speaks briefly but intensely about the dangers to young Black men on the streets of our city, in the classrooms of our schools. When it is my turn, I continue the story, telling about how often Khary is stopped and asked to present his identification card at the New England college he attends; how several weeks before his friend was presumed to be a thief and arrested for riding his own bike at night; how frightened and angry I am. I tell of these dangers some of our sons are living with every day. I talk about a generation of Black children in American schools, sacrificed by neglect and the great pathology of racism to the destruction of guns and drugs; about the recently reported statistic that by the year 2000 one out of three young Black men will be in American prisons. I speak with Khary's voice in my head: *If this were happening to white American boys, would no one care? Would they talk only of building more prisons and killing people in the electric chair?* I hear a man's voice, a boy's voice, and I hear, like notes from a musical instrument slightly out of tune, the high and low tones mixing and alternating during the months when his voice changed from a boy's into a man's.

Feeling like some weird, modern, female version of the ancient mariner, I have been recounting this story whenever I can, trying to convey some of the alarm I feel all around me. We cannot continue to ignore all that we ignore, I say. There is the requirement to remember, which also means to see, and in seeing to act. Silently, I retrieve fragments of Jewish tradition to keep back the fear that I might be thought of as intrusive by some, speaking irrelevancies. I think of the Stranger in Jewish law as Rachel described it in that sermon years before and of Rachel, the rabbi, being treated like a stranger herself; of Elijah's place at the table; of the tradition of the Jewish storyteller, like my father, who when asked a philosophical or moral question would often begin Let me tell you a story.

After the blindness of whiteness is gone, the time of passing over begins. Blackness is. There is no escape in a world which everywhere has made color a sign of caste. But skin which is various shades of brown is still only skin which is various shades of brown. Imagine the grace of that ordinary enlightenment ending the great evil of color and culture re-made into race. I think of Adam and Khary as children, before they knew the difference; of my white niece, Gabrielle, who when she was seven years old and told that Douglas and I were an "interracial" couple, asked, which one is white? I think of Douglas's childhood, and of Lois's, cen-trally constructed around the need to fight off injustice and create a sense of pride. Every single day, again and again and again.

But I am thinking also of all I have learned from Black literature and from my family about survival and resistance, about the long haul of internal liberation, about the need for many voices and memories work-ing together to narrate the past, a story Black writers have told with exquisite precision, a finely tuned perfection that has been necessary in order to survive. Paying the price of the ticket and understanding the meaning of the blues. In my long journey of escape from the whiteness of whiteness, I have come upon a piece of understanding of the blackness of Blackness after all.

As I speak at that recent Seder, I look over at Douglas and see the tears I am just barely resisting filling his eyes. I think of the story of the biblical Ruth who became part of the Jews through love of her mother-in-law, and who at the moment of her decision spoke words I might say to my sons, Douglas and his family, the community and history to which they belong: *Entreat me not to leave thee or to return from following after thee: for whither thou goest, I will go, whither thou lodgest, I will lodge: thy people shall be my people, and thy God my God.*

Words that suggest a myth that might change the world.

FOUR.

REUNIONS,

RETELLINGS,

REFRAINS

The "placeless" . . . are translators of the nontraditional . . . their lineage is fluid,
nomadic, transitional. Their appropriate mark is a crossing sign at the junction.
— Houston A. Baker, Jr., Blues, Ideology and Afro-American Literature

August, 1994: Topsail Beach, North Carolina

I am sitting several feet from the ocean in front of a house our family
has rented for a week's vacation preceding a formal reunion of Douglas's
father's extended kin. The house is perfect in size and design, with four
bedrooms, two on each side of a long kitchen/living room, affording
privacy yet assuring connection. Our bedroom and Lois's face the water,
each with its own screen door through which I can not only hear the
ocean but see it first thing in the morning; and because of the long, lit up
fishing pier nearby, I can also see the silvery white foam of the waves any

time I wake in the night. Ordinarily disturbing nighttime wakefulness is transformed, here, into a gift: the recurring rhythms of the waves, the pier lights, the moonlight on the water.

Battered, rusty screen doors admit sea winds into all the rooms. Other than the safety of our shelter, then, it is as if we are actually living on the beach. I think frequently of my sister, my niece, my closest friends, all people who feel an immediate interior calm near the ocean, and I wish they were all here with me now.

On a tattered rope stretched between two posts on the front porch, our damp towels and clothing hang from weathered, wooden clothespins. We sit in old wooden or plastic chairs on the long length of grey porch, our feet propped on the railing, reading, talking, staring at the horizon, or at Khary and his Great-uncle Sim, who are fishing on the shore. You can walk for miles in either direction, from one pier to the next, and even though houses crowd the dunes and reach back into the town in three or four layers, the beach itself always seems empty.

I am rarely without my notebook on this family vacation. I want to record the recovery of history symbolized by family reunion, to try to understand my place within it. For the second time we have come to celebrate the continuity of family and to acknowledge with our own rituals the tragedies of recent deaths. The story of my education as an American woman into a perspective of Blackness has gone through numerous cycles by now, and in many ways the journey is achieved. Yet, each time I return to North Carolina, home to at least four known generations on both sides of Douglas's family, I am reminded of the unending paradox of exile and belonging, one clear place where my individual history and African American life converge. The notebook serves this second function as well, then. It is a shield against feeling out of place, a visible sign of my journey and the ground writing has always been for me.

I watch the ocean roll and drift during these five days of respite before the family visits begin, and I am drawn into the water many times a day, as if only there can I find peace of mind, a freedom from the demand of turning impressions and feelings into words. Then, propelled to move again by restless consciousness, I return to the shore, pick up my journal and resume making notes.

After the flight from New York to Raleigh-Durham, we had driven two hours from the airport, stopping along the way to eat barbeque — vinegared slivers of roasted pork — which is not as delicious as I remembered. This disappointment is due not to some nostalgic culinary illusion but to a widely reported downsliding in the restaurant fare. Indeed, the homemade food I will eat in the next few days — onion-smothered pork and beef, macaroni and cheese, sweetened corn — will taste as irresistible as ever; no amount of overloaded fat content can prevent me from stuffing myself to the gills.

We have come still raw from our most recent family tragedy, the death of Douglas's brother Simeon who several months before succumbed to AIDS-related viruses. As we gather now, we gathered then, around his bed during the final days of his dying, our own family circle encircled closely by his friends, a community of experienced sufferers in San Francisco, where he lived. Sheets and towels were washed daily. Casseroles and salads, breads and drinks and cakes were brought in a steady stream. Notebooks were kept religiously: doses of medicines; phone numbers of doctors and services; instructions of what to do and where to call when death finally comes. Some of his ashes were scattered in the Pacific he loved, and we have brought the remainder to this beach where he spent many childhood days with his parents, his two brothers, and his sister.

Simeon is the second brother in the family to die young. The first, Ricky, Lois's eldest child, died more than ten years before, and Frederick, their father, eight years before that. Each time we come down for a reunion or family visit, we must also reunion with the dead, visiting the graves of father and brother, placing flowers around the stones, whispering messages which may — we hope for a moment — be carried from spirit to spirit across borders far more inscrutable than any I am considering in this meditation. Now we shall have to visit this ocean each time as well, walking into the waters at a certain spot where we will remember Simeon.

His ashes are preserved in an African basket which Lois has carried from West Coast to East, now to the South and home. The rest of us wait for her signal that the right moment has come to scatter them in the sea. Now Douglas is the only man left in the immediate family. No brothers left, he keeps saying, as if this altered reality is as great as the searing loss of beloved individuals.

Yet, there are still seven of us, and we gather here on the North Carolina coast, excited by the thought of all the relations traveling back to Kinston, Douglas's hometown, many to meet each other for the first time. Somehow, we have all arranged to be here—Adam from Los Angeles, Tiffani, Ricky's daughter, who has just returned from a cross-country trip, the rest of us from New York. Throughout the week, as we talk of politics, of family relationships, of the irresistible taste of high fat, unhealthy foods, I keep on hearing Simeon's voice, fierce, mocking, and tender.

We had expected to be in the Black community, about a mile up the beach where we have always stayed before, but now we realize very quickly that everyone around us is white. Lois tells us not to worry despite the long and recent history of complete segregation on southern beaches like this one. "I told the realtor," she assures us; "Not only are we a Black family, we are an interracial family. And I don't want any mess. I told her if there is any mess, I'll be ready for it." The realtor was solicitous over the phone, then when we arrived to pick up the sheets, towels, and key, but I cannot really imagine anyone intentionally messing with Lois. Racially, everything on the surface seems changed. Douglas and I walk down the beach and do not seem to attract a glance. One day he returns from the grocery store and tells us the white saleswoman turned to him and the white woman behind him on line and asked, "Are you together?" And the woman responded flirtatiously, "Not in this life, but maybe in the next." Everyone seems to make a point of addressing Douglas as "sir," and this, though reassuring, makes him feel old.

"Pleasant manners, amiable sociability, folksy charm, public access everywhere for blacks and whites,"[1] as John Edgar Wideman describes this "new South." "Could the changes I observe," he wonders, "really be as drastic, as swift and final as they seem? Could the turnaround really have been as easy as it appears, the black-white divide like some terrible pestilence, killing, afflicting tens of thousands for centuries, then a cure discovered, a vaccine, and most people are inoculated. One generation and the bad old days just a bad old memory?"[2]

One day while Douglas is walking up the beach with Khary and Adam, a young white boy throws some stones at him. Douglas looks around and sees that everyone nearby is white. Nevertheless, he approaches one of the men and tells him what happened. "Your child deliberately threw stones at me," Douglas says. The man is extravagantly apologetic, even placing his hand tentatively on Douglas's arm. The child is not his, he says, but he knows the parents. He will tell them. He apologizes again, pointedly calling Douglas "sir." But the child remains silent, staring at them from a few feet away. Was he being merely mischievous, badly behaved, with no attention to racial differences? Or was he expressing with naked, childlike openness, the actual family feeling? Was the adult genuine in his apology, or only avoiding trouble in a way more common now than the open confrontations of ten years before? There is no way of knowing for sure, but Douglas's life spans a generation between strict segregation and this new ambiguous transition in the midst of a nation turning dramatically, increasingly to the right. How much can be covered over in ten, twenty years?

"Isn't it ungenerous," Wideman asks ironically, "for a guest who's been served a delicious meal to peek under the tablecloth for crumbs, search for ancient blood stains on the floor. How long? How long?"[3]

Sixteen generations of Black Americans lived in slavery or enforced legal segregation. Only one and a half generations have lived since Brown v. Board of Education *struck down the legalities of separate facilities in institutions of all kinds.*

Most days we walk the mile to the Black community where it is unquestionably more comfortable, as if a layer of wariness has been stripped away. I keep imagining those clear plastic poster frames covered with layers of thin acetate, and each time you peel off a layer of supposedly transparent plastic, the poster underneath gets clearer until you can see through it as well as if there were nothing covering it at all. We feel uncovered up at the Black part of the beach, our bodies stripped open to the sun. The beach is a bit wilder there, the grasses more beautiful, the dunes higher. A graceful cove shapes the sand where it meets the pier.

On that pier, four years before, I was suddenly white and cold as ice as I walked ahead of my family, seemingly alone, when a Black man grabbed my breast, sneered, then sauntered away. It happened so quickly I stood motionless for a moment, in shock. By the time Douglas, Adam and Khary rushed up to me, the man was halfway down the pier, and when he saw them surround me, that I was with them, he disappeared. I was relieved that I had been alone in case one of them had taken it into his head to "defend" me, threatening a fight. At the same time, I wished I knew enough self-defense to knock him out where he stood. When the suggestion to return to Topsail came up, I was reluctant at first, afraid I'd feel restrained about walking alone on the beach, one of my greatest pleasures in life. Yet, now I am surprised to discover I too am more comfortable on this end of the beach, not only because Lois believes that the experience was an aberration and is unlikely to occur again, but because — I realize with some surprise — whiteness has come to intimidate me more than Blackness. "At least you can go out alone whenever you want," Douglas teases me now when I go for my morning swim and walk on the white side. I smile, feeling a mixture of unpleasant comfort and familiar discomfort as I walk out alone to blend in. In my journal I write: It seems I have grown used to this dissonance between my actual skin and myself.

The first time I came down South, more than twenty years before, I was repeatedly mistaken for a very light-skinned Black woman who had lived in Kinston when Douglas and his siblings were growing up. "Are you Susie Porter?" a white waitress asked. "Well, honey, you must be Susie

Porter," a white saleswoman declared as I slipped in and out of their categories. I am sure I looked nothing like Susie Porter, but I was surrounded by Black people, obviously a member of a Black family, and
therefore I had to be "Black." Now, my grey hair, which can look
tannish-blond in some light, makes me less racially ambiguous. And being middle-aged confuses even more. I am more clearly a white woman
with a Black man, yet that combination is associated with a kind of
tabooed, threatening and titilating sexuality reserved in most of our
minds for the young. Here are two grey-haired people with their obviously shared, grown sons, a suggestion of abiding love which perhaps
can be more disturbing to our prejudices even than forbidden sexual
desire.

One day two Black men appear on the beach in front of our house
while Khary and I are swimming. Lois begins talking loudly to me from
the porch. I remember my first trip to Kinston when she repeatedly
introduced me to neighbors as "my girl," a code signifying her approval
of Douglas's marriage, and I immediately understand that she is formally
establishing that I am "with" the Black people, not just happening to be
swimming next to a young Black man.

But Lois explains to me anyway as soon as she reaches the edge of the
water: "The reason I said that was so they would know for sure you're
with us and not try any funny stuff."

I nod, wait for her typical repetition of crucial information: "You hear
me? I didn't want any funny stuff. So I talked to you real loud so they'd
know for sure you were with us."

Most whites living in a white community would never admit to so
continuous a consciousness of color. Many overtly racist whites will
insist that "race" is irrelevant to their views, translating their insistence
on racial divisions into coded phrases such as: we all want to stick to our
own. Trained to the privilege of normalcy, even progressive whites are
often shocked to learn of the constant vigilance about color and race
among Black people whenever white people are around. There are certainly times when I grow weary of it, even now thinking (hoping?) that
perhaps Lois or the others are exaggerating the situation. But then I

recall a Black friend who, one day when we were walking and talking of the racial problems in the city, suddenly shouted to the sky, "My god, I am so sick of this, fighting this all of my life, knowing I will never experience a time when I don't have to think about race every single day." I remember my Black student telling the largely white class, You think you are tired of talking about race? Think of how I feel.

In these matters of race consciousness and Black pride, of wariness and readiness for battle, Lois's ability to win out over fate and survive dire social conditions, are famous. Once, waiting for admission to an emergency room when Simeon was sick, she told me bluntly: "Go tell them we've been here for hours. They'll believe you cause you're white." She is a resistance fighter at heart and by necessity. I obey her, resent her, tease her, am angry or grateful or frustrated and always full of admiration.

Her father, Isaac, was killed by lightning, dead before she, his seventh child, was born. By the time she was five, her mother, Sally, was dead from pneumonia. Their last photograph hangs on Lois's bedroom wall. A tall, dark man with deep-set eyes, wearing a suit which seems too tight around his neck, sits beside a fair-skinned woman, her straight hair pulled into a neat roll around her head, a long, high-necked dress reaching up to her chin in a border of lace.

"On the night of Isaac's death," we were told by a cousin on one of our visits South, "Sally gathered the children in fear of the storm, telling them to be still. She said, 'Shhhh, chi-in,' she couldn't take the time to say chillin. Storm must have been coming from two sides, cause we couldn't walk." The cousin, well into her eighties then, seemed to visualize the night as clearly as she saw us all sitting there, gathered around her in her small living room, her head leaned forward from the back of a newly covered chair, her hand, even though she was sitting, resting heavily on a cane. "I remember that storm, the three of us children together couldn't shut the door, the wind was so strong. Isaac's head was falling off his neck when they got to him. There was a dark brown spot where the lightning hit."

The younger children were taken in by various aunts and uncles after the parents' deaths, but eventually the elder brothers and sister reunited the family. They lived in a house built by their father on land owned by their grandfather, Balaam Meadows, who lived the first part of his life in slavery, then was freed during the Civil War. The house is still lived in by another of Lois's brothers, whom we will visit later in the week. By the time Lois and her husband, Frederick, were twenty-one, both had dropped out of high school to raise their children. Somehow, between the money Frederick won gambling and his fierce loyalty, and Lois's proud, uncompromised devotion, they brought all four children through their college years.

I'd heard these stories ever since I entered the family in 1968. But it was only at Lois's family reunion, four years before this one of Douglas's father's side, that the history took on a vivid and intense life for me. Like any story I have read and loved and soon begin to feel I somehow possess, Douglas's family stories have taken up permanent residence in my imagination — that *place* in me where images feel as solid as an old wooden table in the family for years, as real as the story of my father's mother, the grandmother I never knew, hiding and protecting her children from pogroms in Kishenev, a place I have never seen. The stories of my in-laws are part of the context of my sense of who I am. When I came South with my family for the Meadows reunion, it became clear to me that the history that helped to create the life stories of my children had strongly marked me as well.

August, 1990:

We board a train and head south in the opposite direction of the great Black migrations I have recently been reading about in my ongoing studies of African American literature.

From Toni Morrison's *Jazz:*

"Eager, a little scared, they did not even nap during the fourteen hours of a ride smoother than a rocking cradle. The quick darkness in the carriage cars when they shot through a tunnel made them wonder if maybe there was a wall ahead to crash into or a cliff hanging over nothing. The train shivered with them at the thought but went on and sure enough there was ground up ahead and the trembling became the dancing under their feet."[4]

From Houston Baker's *Blues, Ideology and Afro-American Literature:*

"The crossing-sign is the antithesis of a place marker. It signifies always, change, motion, transience, process. To adept adherents of wandering, a crossing sign is equivalent to a challenge thrown out in brash, sassy tones by a locomotive blowing by: 'Do what you can,' it demands. 'Do what you can — right here — on this placeless-place, this spotless-spot — to capture manifold intonations and implications of fluid experience!'"[5]

I feel more than the phrase *thinking about* history implies, more than the idea even of *recollection* conveys, as I read paragraphs about trains and traveling collected in my journal over time. It is more like I am remembering, as if beloved passages from fiction, images in film and old photographs, partial lyrics from countless blues about traveling and moving on are as real as the steady beat of the wheels on the tracks, the call of the whistle as we move out of the dark tunnels surrounding Pennsylvania Station and head into the open. As we begin our journey south, I think about the Underground Railroad too, the railroad as symbol and reality of Black people moving toward freedom.

"I was making my way to the land where the ground still runs red with the blood of African Americans. The land where the trees still stand from which Black men were lynched. The land where the air still rings with the echo of slavery," Khary writes in his own narrative of this journey. "I thought of my family's stories of segregation, Jim Crow, and the old south. I thought of my family."[6] And again, as when I was in the Richmond Museum, Jewish and Black experience converge as I recall stories told to me by Jewish friends who visited the sites of concentration camps in Poland and Germany.

Lois and her brother, Alphonso, sit together; in front of them Douglas's sister, Sherrill, and Tiffani. Adam and Khary are across from them, Douglas and I farther up the aisle. Despite the sorrow and loss which has been part of every family occasion for years because of our dead, we are excited and inspired by the efforts of several old women — in their late seventies and early eighties — who have made this reunion happen through their letters, calls, meticulous organization. They searched throughout the country for the scattered descendants of Balaam and Caroline Meadows who had been liberated from slavery during the Civil War and died in the 1930s in Trenton, North Carolina where they had raised children and grandchildren on their own land.

In Rocky Mount, where we will disembark and pick up a van for the drive to Trenton, we will also meet Douglas's brother Simeon, who is coming from the West Coast.

Between New York's Pennsylvania Station and Philadelphia, passing by the wide highways of New Jersey, the bleak poverty of Newark, I am remembering from my own childhood numerous weekend trips with my sister and father to his first American home in North Philadelphia where his three sisters still lived in the then Jewish, now almost entirely Black, neighborhood of Strawberry Mansion. Only two hours south, the journey seemed grand and adventurous then. Perched on our suitcases with my sister, as my father went off to purchase the tickets, then riding to this same background music of train whistles and the steady beat of the engine, those sounds became the archetypal sound of any journey for me. In Philadelphia, we were in a new world, that is to say an old world where my father's relatives spoke Yiddish as often as English; where my uncles operated shops in front of their houses — one sold jewelry, the other made quilts; where my aunts fixed noodles stuffed with raisins and nuts, meat cooked and softened for hours in dark gravies. For my father, they extracted large bones with little but gristle left on them which he noisily sucked dry, sighing in mysterious ecstacy.

Once outside of Philadelphia, we are truly heading south, eventually into Washington, D.C. Arriving at this station always reminds me of demonstrations; of rising at 4 A.M. to board a bus or a train to the capital where we marched for integration, against the war in Vietnam, against apartheid in South Africa. In 1963, I came to Washington with a friend and, after marching, singing, and shouting for hours, I fell asleep in the sun. Suddenly, my friend was shaking me, and I woke to hear the sounds of King's resonant sermon, words about dreams and freedom which over the next twenty-five years would sear into the American consciousness with increasingly fragile hope. I have never forgotten that moment of waking up to his voice, its echo through the microphone over the heads of the crowd of thousands — and feeling: *this is history, history is here, in this place right now, and I am here too.* Somewhere in that crowd Douglas and his family clapped and shouted as I was doing, but it would be some time before our histories would meet at a crossroad of our lives.

Further south, we travel through woods, meadows, farmlands, and I am seeing Nell and Helene, from Toni Morrison's *Sula,* squatting with other Black women in the fields when the trains stop for them to "relieve themselves," forbidden to use the bathrooms on the trains or in the stations which are reserved for whites.

"Was that still going on in the 1940s?" I asked Lois recently when I wondered if she remembered this indignity from her trips on the train from South to North and back again. "No," she says. "They had colored bathrooms on the train by then." I turn my head away, ashamed even to watch her remember.

We pick up the van in Rocky Mount, and head first to Kinston, where Douglas and his siblings were born. Uncle Alphonso begins the story of their grandmother's shack, the one insulated with newspapers the youngsters read and reread since they didn't have any books. *How come you can read Grandmammie?* As Alphonso repeats the question, retelling the often-told story to remind us of history, I wait as eagerly as I did the first time for her answer, as though I have not heard it before. Or, perhaps my excitement derives from having heard the story so many times it has become like a known rendition of some jazz or blues structure whose very predictability intensifies its meaning and its emotion. ("Listen to this phrase one more time," Adam will say about some piece of music he loves — "Just one more time, Mom." And as it plays over and over, the music gets into his shoulders, which move back and forth, his feet, which beat a rhythm on the floor, his face, which breaks into a smile.) *Because I was in the house,* Alphonso says, then pauses and begins to explain the meaning of his grandmother's statement to the younger generation who listen attentively although, in their late teens and early twenties, they have also heard the story many times and understand the connection between reading and being "in the house." "You see, house slaves were often the children of masters, or favored in some other way," Alphonso says. Adam, Khary, and Tiffani look at each other and smile. When the story is finished, Adam clap-drums a slow, even beat on his thighs. Then, after a pause, calls out *mmmm, hmmm. Yeah.*

When we reach Kinston, it is decided we will take a quick tour, and Lois and Alphonso, now joined by Douglas, point out significant family places and events beginning with Mitchell Wooten Courts, the project where Lois's children were raised. "People up north always look kind of sympathetic when we talk about living in the project," she tells us as we slowly round the small streets that separate the red brick row houses, still home to many Black families in the town. "But at that time it was a great thing to get an apartment in the project. We were the lucky ones. We had running water, and heat in the winter, and my children could roam free all around the place, knew everyone around." This, too, we have all been told before, and like the rest of the story it intrigues us again. We even find new questions to ask, or else we repeat old ones, just to keep the story going on. Adam, Khary, Tiffani and I look out the windows of the van like tourists in some exotic yet familiar land as Douglas points out the woods he set fire to when he was a little boy, then was beaten for. "You weren't beaten so badly, boy," Lois tells him now, chuckling. In ordinary life, in New York City where we all live, she rarely calls her oldest living son *boy.* It is an endearment he responds to with his own part in the long rehearsed family dialogue. "That's just cause I was too fast for Daddy. I didn't stand there and scream like Ricky or Simmie. I ran under the bed where he couldn't get me."

We pass Adkin, the old Black high school now boarded up and closed. Behind it is a modern gym, rebuilt after a fire which was rumored to have been started purposely by Blacks so the town would have to build a new one. Small children are running around the sidewalks and yards, standing in screen doors staring out at us, as Douglas must once have done.

Later that week, visiting the old friends and relatives who live in this part of Kinston, some of them still in the project, we will hear of the differences from the 1950s when Douglas grew up here. Miss Charlotte will tell us how you can't go out anymore at night because of drugs. The dealers and addicts sit right on her front lawn, and no one would dare tell them to move. Douglas's Aunt Nannie, in her eighties then, will tell us, as we sit in her immaculate living room, filled with spotless rugs and lace curtains, crystal vases and ashtrays on each of the highly polished end tables, that she nails her windows down, keeps the fan going summer and winter for air, never, never goes out for a walk after dark.

Riding through the streets of Kinston, I remember the first time I visited, when Lois and Frederick still lived there and I was pregnant with Adam. It was the first time I experienced the ritual I have now grown used to. We will visit all the relatives and friends each time we come home, even if the occasion for our trip is a funeral. Taking several days, if necessary, we will make the rounds from house to house. There is no calling in advance to arrange times or even days. But the word has gotten around. Lois is in town with her family and they will be coming by.

Each time we visit the same people, marking the changes in their lives as they mark ours. We visit Mr. and Mrs. Newberne and their son Lee, who has survived for more than two decades a kidney disease that would have long since killed a weaker man. Each year the doctors predict he will die soon. "When I get tired of fighting, then I'll go," he tells us matter-of-factly for nearly two decades. Their road is still dry dirt, even after years of county promises to pave it, but the small house exudes a luxurious feeling created, I think, by the intensity of easily expressed love. "I would be dead without my Mama," Lee tells us each time. "They told me I'd be dead twenty years ago, but she keeps me going on." A thoroughgoing survivor like her friend Lois, Mrs. Newberne, alone among the many sufferers from "sugar" diabetes we meet, is neither defeated nor victimized by the disease. "Diabetes can be controlled, but *you* have to control it," she tells us in contrast to all the others who insist they are eating "healthy" vegetables which are seasoned with sugar, a healthy "fruit dessert" which is smothered in sweet whipped cream. Mr. Newberne, a small and stocky man, lays his head on Douglas's chest when we prepare to leave and, tears gathering in his eyes, says hoarsely, "I love you, boy. I sure am glad you came by."

We drive past the Harlem Inn Cafe, once owned by Lois's brother Fulton, now boarded up like many of the other stores downtown which, as in so many small American cities, have been forced out of business by the huge shopping malls which sprawl on the outskirts, leaving the center of town desolate and empty, another haven for drug dealers. But most of the sights pointed out to us during the half hour it takes to make our way through town are related to the early civil rights movement in which Douglas and his family, lead by Simeon who was then a high school student, were centrally involved. We ride past the white movie theater they couldn't attend, past the restaurants and drug store counters where they demonstrated and sat-in during the period which, Douglas has told us numerous times, was one of the turning points of his life, a time of resistance, of suddenly expanded possibilities.

Back on the road to Trenton, we pass a small field lined with houses, and in the center of the field is a small shack, its wooden planks beginning to disintegrate, its door boarded shut. This is the house of Lois's maternal grandmother, but we do not stop due to lack of time, promising ourselves to do so on the way back to Kinston, or on our next trip south. By the time we are ready, four years later, on our way to another reunion of the other branch of the family, the house will be gone, replaced by a series of newly built homes, the half-empty field now a crowded acre of small buildings: a new neighborhood.

Trenton, a town formed in 1784, has always had a substantial Black population. We stop for a moment at Brock Mill Pond, a body of water "probably built by slaves," one of the local history books reports parenthetically amid the hundreds of pages devoted entirely to white history of the town. The silver blue-gray water is surrounded by overhanging cypress trees which are shrouded in Spanish moss. The moss hangs low, nearly touching the opaque water, like veils of history, hiding and protecting truths we are too timid or too cruel to remember.

Onto the corner of Cherry and Trent roads, we enter the land once lived on by Balaam, approach the old family house now occupied by one of his grandsons, Lois's brother, Lionel. He is sitting on the front porch and doesn't move when we enter his yard, standing by the van doors until Lois and Alphonso emerge and lead the way to the porch. Alphonso sits down next to his brother, whom he hasn't seen in years, and neither of them speaks. The rest of us stand around near the porch as Lois points out the road to the left which later on we will take to the graveyard. And still, the two men are quiet. When they finally begin speaking, it is as if they left off the day before yesterday. The love is obviously deep and powerful, yet no one would express it in word or touch. I marvel at this difference from the old world Jewish culture I remember from Philadelphia where the hugging and kissing hello, accompanied by vociferous tears and loud proclamations in Yiddish of yearnings now finally brought to an end took nearly an hour to complete. This difference between Douglas's family and mine which has found its entrenched way into both our personalities, has been a source of trouble between us over the years. But now I am thinking, in comparison with his uncles, how noisy and expressive he is. "Talk about progress," he says, scratching his ear, when I read him these lines.

We are standing around the yard, glancing across a narrow road to another house, when a white man emerges and heads toward us. He bounds over to Lois and shakes her hand vigorously asking, "Ain't you Lois? I ain't seen you in fifty years! You and I used to play together in this yard, remember?" She is gracious, says yes, she does, but later admits she has only a vague memory of some white boy of five or six years old coming over to play with her. The white man's memory, of one little Black girl, liked though forbidden as a serious friend, is strikingly different from the Black woman's memory whose interstices are crowded with white faces both friendly and unfriendly, who had to be read with precision and care to mark the proper rules for interaction and thus self-protection.

Finally, Lois pushes her brother's shoulder and says, "Well, aren't you going to invite us inside?" He rises, laughing and motioning us with a stretched-out hand, and they lead us into their childhood home. For

Lionel, of course, who lives here, this is an ordinary visit. For those of us who have never been here before, it is as if we are entering an ancient site, filled with living meaning.

We enter the room where Lois was born and I stop to stare at the corner of the room where she points and says, "Right there." We move to the kitchen where she and Alphonso repeatedly stole their mothers' pies from off the low window sill. Outside, the house is newly painted white, black shutters shining like dark spots in a brilliant sun. But inside the house is old, walls and floors as they must have been for nearly 100 years. Doorways are low, window sills so close to the floor they hit you on the knees. A mantle piece is crowded with photographs, including one of Aunt Marie, the eldest sister who functioned as mother to the rest, who by now has arrived from New Orleans and sits on the front porch with two of her brothers.

Sally's photograph is on the mantle piece, and I will see it in small guilded frames on many end tables and mantle pieces as we travel from house to house. The daughter of Sophie, the grandmother of the newspaper-lined shack, her skin is fair, her hair piled neatly on top of her head as it is in the photograph with her husband I have seen many times on Lois's wall. Her distinctive, large eyes with nearly invisible lids are reflected in the large eyes of many of her children and grandchildren. This recognition of physical features, large eyes, a turn of the cheekbone, a singular posture or way of holding the hands will be a recurring motif during the day of the actual reunion. I will look around the large community center at the hundreds of strangers and see Adam's jaw line, the arch of Khary's brows.

Endless teasing by the men of each other evokes unstated affection confirmed by a certain kind of laugh. One woman releases a shared memory from the forgotten past, and another woman responds, "Yes, honey," or "Yes, Lord," narrating the enduring and endearing ties of kin. More recently acquired habits of speech and gesture seem to be falling away from Lois and Douglas. Words take on a longer, broader twang. Even Khary and Adam seem to be developing a slightly new pronunciation for some of their words. *Mom,* is more often becoming *Mama*. I hear *ain't* more than usual, and *Hey, how you doin,* with a certain down-beat on the *do.*

When Adam returns to the yard, he picks up his guitar and begins to sing a familiar blues song. A crowd of small children gathers around him. They lean over his shoulders, sit between his knees. One insists on sitting on his lap behind the guitar, helping to pluck the strings.

Stranger, in-law, and the only white person around, I hang out with Adam, gaining a comforting reminder from the fluid identities he loves. As I watch my sons surrounded by their family, I am aware of our differences but also of our ties. When I look over at Khary, who is alternating between taking photographs and asking a million questions of his various relatives, I think about our mutual, long involvement in Black literature. I remember taking him to his first poetry reading in Harlem, a protest against apartheid where he purchased a poster demanding the release of Nelson Mandela which still hangs on his wall. I think of how similar I am to this son who identifies so strongly with his Blackness. Then, as I hear his relentless questioning of his uncles and aunts, I recall a famous story of Douglas's childhood, how he asked so many questions his godmother would sometimes draw her curtains, anticipating weariness, when she saw him coming down the road. *Mixed bloods.* Common blood, I think, is the more accurate phrase, and I remember my father's chant of reclamation whenever I thought myself too different from him: "My blood is coursing through your veins," he would shout, pointing at me like some overwrought Hebrew prophet. "And don't you forget it, old girl!"

As always, everyone is especially warm to me, and there are those, like Uncle Alphonso and Aunt Marie, to whom I have been close now for many years. I feel welcomed by this family I became part of twenty-five years before, by all Lois's cousins, who begin to crowd the driveway, the women providing the embraces and long, repeated kisses I had missed before. "Come on, you can hug me too," I am told if I am shy or hold back for a moment. It is not the cultural difference from myself that is the source of my restraint. I am thinking about all the meanings of mixed family lines and common blood. My children have a heritage which is not my heritage, a legacy which is not my own. They are me and not me, mine and not mine. I am a stranger, yet I also belong and that combination feels suddenly suitable, familiar, and fine.

Perhaps noticing me standing on the outskirts, Lois grabs my arm. She takes me through all the rooms upstairs, pointing out an old brass bed, a worn but graceful tall, wooden dresser with an attached mirror framed in intricately carved dark wood. "This would go for thousands on Columbus Avenue," she says, pushing me conspiratorially on the arm.

In the afternoon, we head down the road to a large community center and the reunion itself. Most of the families of the children of Balaam Meadows and Caroline Williams Meadows are represented. We take our places at long, cafeteria-style tables and attend to the first speaker who reads from First Corinthians.

"Though I speak with the tongues of men and angels, and have not charity, I am become as sounding brass, or a tinkling cymbal.

"And though I have the gift of prophesy, and understand all mysteries and all knowledge; and though I have all faith, so that I could remove mountains, and have not charity, I am nothing."[7]

I first read these words carefully while teaching a course in contemporary women's literature, especially in relation to Toni Morrison's novels where First Corinthians is read and reread over time and through many different interpretations. But I have also come to understand the words very personally. Perhaps I have even appropriated and decontextualized them, but for me the passage seems to say something about being an artist and being a mother. As a young mother, it was clear to me very early that if I had to model my life on the image of the great, male genius — selfish, self-involved and steeped always in his own sacred mysteries, unsuited by virtue of his talent to the mundane demands and expectations of ordinary life — then I could be no artist at all. My small children's lives were too compelling to ignore, my passion for them too great to exile them to the periphery of my consciousness. Yet, I knew it would be crippling to give up the life of a working writer. Economic considerations aside for the moment (I also had to earn money), the only possible resolution for me was to attempt to redefine what it meant to be an artist and the material from which she drew her work. It was then I began to see that a central conflict of motherhood — the tension between obligations to others and obligations to the self — was also an essential human conflict which could be placed at a crossroads of the artist's journey. The two lines of the crossroads would read artist and mother for me, and in the center I would stand, learning and relearning a balance that seemed increasingly possible, if only by necessity, a motif by which I could understand the conflicts of my days. Charity (giving to others) would eat me up alive, as it had generations of women, without the solitude to see as fully and honestly as I could into the truth of my experience and write about what I found there. But prophesy (my work) would become vacuous without charity (my need to love). Writing about motherhood became a central subject for me, a story within which I could trace this human dilemma of the boundaries and pathways between self and others throughout the development of my children's lives. There were plenty of blues along the way, a trouble in mind that sat down in my house on intimate terms with me. But there were few shallow sounds of tinkling cymbals as I joined the effort of women to rewrite the portrait of the artist, this time as a young, aging, and old woman.

Undoubtedly, it was coincidental that these of all words were spoken at the opening of the reunion where I sat among over a hundred relatives, my notebook open in my lap. But at that moment my life seemed to knit together, its separate challenges finding a coherence beyond words, a unity as formidable as the faces of generations all around me, the descendants of Balaam and Caroline Meadows. I received that occasional gift, felt that old treasured "moment of being" of Virginia Woolf's, when you discover a "pattern beneath appearances," a "sense of what belongs to what."[8]

After the reading from the bible, one of the eldest cousins tells the audience that the saddest thing that happened in the family was Isaac's and Sally's early deaths, and we are comforted as what we have always thought of as a personal tragedy is embraced by the extended kin. Many people who speak are in tears. Aunt Marie stands and holds out her arms silently. When she can find her voice she says, "You have extended my years." And then a song, lead by the generation of Lois's parents and cousins who have created this event: "I sing because I'm happy. I sing because I'm free."

Each family "head," in our case first Aunt Marie, then Lois, then each of the surviving brothers, stands to speak and introduce their own families. Then, each of us, including me, must stand individually and have our names spoken out loud. Douglas's generation. Adam's and Khary's. The small children who are running in and out of the aisles between the tables. Each person rises when his or her name is called and kin relationship identified.

A man of about seventy introduces himself as an illegitimate son of Balaam, rejected by the legitimate family until very recently. Physically, he could be the father of Simeon. He has the same facial structure, the same slightly exotic look always called "kind of Eastern" in the family. Perhaps, I think, this is the facial structure that comes from Balaam.

I look at their photograph now, as I write these words. The older man's arm curves around Simeon who looks at him with a warm, slightly startled smile.

On the beach in Topsail four years later, I spend a lot of time thinking about Simeon. When I first came into the family, we were very close, two of a kind, according to the others. They meant, I think, we were both passionate and convinced, to a virtue and to a fault. He was a Vietnam draft resistor, a leader of the civil rights movement and, soon after he came out as gay to his family, a leader of the gay movement as well. Never patient with hypocrisy of any kind, he sent an open letter to family and friends all over the country, including in Kinston, claiming his identity as a gay man. Like Audre Lorde who wrote of herself as a "Black woman lesbian warrior poet,"[9] he insisted on the inclusiveness of his identity, speaking about his troubles as a Black man in the white, gay movement, his troubles as a gay man in the Black movement.

In recent years, though, we had become distant. I believed his perspective on family matters was always too much that of a son. A child grown into middle age, I thought he kept on seeing his mother only as a mother, responsible for dispensing wisdom, selfless attention, unending strength, with no needs of her own, no ordinary limitations, intractable but forgivable faults. He thought, in part rightly, that I gave insufficient credence to his point of view.

When he discovered that his HIV virus had become full-blown AIDS, he informed Douglas and me first, then planned a trip east to tell Lois. His plan, however, was to tell her in a large group of acquaintances and supporters, and I was horrified. Even then, we fought and argued about the best method of telling a mother what can never, in any circumstances, be anything less than a nightmare for her. But he argued with me because it was my opinion he wanted and trusted. I argued with him because I cared so much what he did, and in the end he complied with my view and told her when they were alone.

He was hospitalized in New York in January 1994, and I walked the snowy streets of Washington Heights to visit him, watching him improve temporarily, hoping against all knowledge that he would defeat the intestinal virus no AIDS patient had ever defeated before. "Simmie!!" I shouted to him once, full of false, determined hope. "Your arms look almost normal size! Your wrists are getting thick again!" He turned his hands around to stare at wasted fingers, called me Sweetie, and smiled.

When he returned to San Francisco with Lois and it became increasingly clear that he would soon die, he called one night to inform me in an irritated tone that we had not cried enough together, not mourned his immanent passing with open enough emotion. That night, both of us sobbed over the long distance telephone wire, talking of how deeply we had affected each others' lives. He made me promise to make sure the family surrounded him right before the end, and when that time came we were all there, accompanying him through his last days.

He lay on a wide bed in a room full of sun, his favorite room in his tiny apartment. He infuriated us all, even then, with his irrational demands, his insistence that he could stand up and take care of himself. I took my turn sitting near him on his bed, stroking his emaciated arms, kissing his cheeks from which the bones protruded like sharp, flat cliffs. I learned, from his friends and the broader community of San Francisco, in a way I had never understood before this direct encounter with AIDS, about the devastations of the disease and about the courage of people who yearly, weekly, sometimes daily, help their friends to die.

I remained in the apartment for hours and days at a time, greeting people, answering phones, gathering the soiled sheets and towels Lois, grim and silent, passed to me like we were on some grotesque assembly line. I ran from the house to the streets of the neighborhood, to the little patio out front, to the grocery store — any place to escape the sounds and smells of impending death. I was angry at him for insisting on dying at home, making us all go through so much. I was proud of him for making us do this, for insisting that we not turn our heads, not close our eyes. I sat by his bed very near the end and rested my head on his skeletal chest. He no longer recognized me, but still seemed to know Lois, Douglas, his sister. Yet, in that moment in the darkening room, I felt his hand squeeze mine, and I hoped perhaps we were remembering our years together, the distance we had traveled and the distances we had known, and that we were reconciled. When he died, in the middle of our seventh night of watching, I was sitting in the adjoining room next to one of his friends. I gasped in shock, as if we had not been waiting for all those days. I went to tell Khary and Tiffani, who after many days of sitting with him, lying near him, helping to care for him, were outside huddled together under an old wool blanket, trying to get some air. They looked like a homeless couple in the cold, March night, and I knew they and the family we belonged to was what I knew best of home. When we returned to Simeon's room, we all gathered in a circle around him. Lois kneeled by his side until Tiffani lifted her up and lead her away. Then, Khary closed his eyes.

During our last days at Topsail Beach, there are mild storms and grey sky but still enough heat to swim in the warm water, rocked by the high, gentle waves. On our last day, Lois tells us it is time, and we walk up the beach to the Black section, her carrying the African basket in her arms.

Seeming to speak to us, her children and grandchildren, from the long line of deaths in her life, from her father Isaac to her son Simeon, she tells us to take a handful of ashes and in any way we wish, give them to the water. She retains one handful in the basket to take home.

Douglas swims way out with his, then dives deep as if planting them in the sea. I swim along the shore, letting them trail slowly out of my fingers, sowing a field. Adam throws them into the sky with his strong quarterback's arm so they arch above us and fall down like rain. Tiffani, Sherrill, and Khary watch us from the shore, then join us to scatter flowers in the water. Some are taken out by the waves. Some are returned to the wet sand.

As always at deaths, Lois insists we take photographs of ourselves. We had come in our clothes, not in bathing suits, and in the photograph we stand huddled together, clutching a few remaining flowers, dripping wet, our eyes looking stunned into the camera. Then, Lois takes the African basket and walks off down the beach alone, a swift nod indicating to us all not to follow her. And I am afraid, watching her walk down the beach, remembering lines from *Jazz:* "'He ain't give you nothing you can't bear, Rose.' But had He? Maybe this one time He had. Had misjudged and misunderstood her particular backbone. This one time. This here particular spine."[10]

She becomes smaller and smaller as she heads toward the next pier, and we finally turn away toward the water, feeling Simeon's presence more tangibly than our own.

And then, a day later, we are on the road to Trenton again, to the old cemetery just around the corner from Lionel's house, past an area called Haitie (pronounced hi-tee) where Lois would be sent as a child to get vegetables, their entire world only several streets, almost all their kin gathered there, their dead buried there as well. The cemetery is in a wide, peaceful meadow surrounded by thick old trees. A path separates the old from the newer graves. Four years before, when we visited this graveyard for the first time, we found Isaac and Sally right away, even Caroline. But there was no immediate sign of Balaam. We all spread out, wandering among the tombstones, mostly of people born into slavery, surviving into the twentieth century, some of them up to 1950. Suddenly, gazing in a kind of trance from stone to stone, I find him. Everyone comes over, grandchildren, great-grandchildren, even this great-granddaughter-in-law, a Jew, one generation out of Eastern Europe, now having contributed her history and genes to the descendants of the rural South, of slavery, of whichever African culture their ancestors were kidnapped from.

"Slavery is not some distant, removed institution," Khary writes in his narrative of the experience. "Here is your gravestone. *Balaam Meadows, born 1838*. I am but four generations removed from slavery. I have returned to pay homage. I am home. *Balaam Meadows, born 1838*. My body is full of your blood."[11]

Later, in a cousin's home, I stare at a drawing of Richard, Balaam's father, looking proud in his tight, dark suit. I think of his son, Balaam, the first Black sheriff of Jones County, look back to the face of his granddaughter, and to her cousin, Lois, daughter of Isaac, and my mother-in-law. In the small, neat room where we all sit in a circle talking and listening, history thickens. The very air seems to support us with presences, something to lean against.

At the reunion of Frederick's family in a Kinston community center, once again we are surrounded by cousins, many of whom have never met each other, some who spent their childhoods running up and down the same roads, eating at whichever house they happened to stop. Once again we see photographs of ancestors: Frederick's grandfather, Alfred; and his father, Fred, a dark, handsome young man with Adam's eyes and mouth, whose photograph hangs on our living room wall; Miss Sylvie, Douglas's grandmother and Fred's wife, whom I have heard about for years but whose face I have never seen. The planes and shapes are familiar, and I suddenly see Khary's full mouth, his narrow dark eyes.

Here again, it is the women, Aunt Mildred, Aunt Bernice, and others, who have created and coordinated the reunion. At a family farm the night before, we had watched as piles of old, brown photographs were arranged on large, white placards, then talked into the night with cousins we hadn't seen in years. Mildred, to whom I always love talking about family history, books, motherhood, is so busy organizing and ordering we barely have time to say hello. But as I watch her face from my seat in the large room, now seeing how much she resembles her mother, Miss Sylvie, I see too that my younger son slightly resembles her. Physical appearance is often unrelated to internal kinship, I think as my eyes move back and forth from Miss Sylvie, to Mildred, to Khary, but sometimes it is. Sometimes it is. When I return home to New York City, I frame a copy of Miss Sylvie's picture for my living room wall.

On our final morning down South, we visit Frederick's and Ricky's graves, as we do each time we come to Kinston. This cemetery is much larger, more modern and urban than the old graveyard in Trenton, and we walk down parallel rows and cement paths, until we find the two tombstones, side by side. Tiffani adjusts the grasses, placing and replacing the flowers we have brought, as if she can make up for the lost years of her father's presence by domestic care of his grave. There is an old Jewish custom of placing a pebble on the tombstone of loved ones, each small stone marking a visit in obedience to the requirement to remember. I explain this tradition to my niece, and we find some small stones which together we place on the marble's edge.

Crossing signs. Paths crossed in space and through the infinite inheritance of time. From the peace of the water to restless consciousness on shore, and back again. Many kinds of journeys fill my imagination — a day, a lifetime, a people moving through history. Pages of a journal turning like ground moving, as if outside the windows of a train.

FIVE.

A COLOR

WITH NO

PRECISE

NAME

"I think I stand on the color line itself, not on one side of it. Or maybe I'm like a bridge stretching across the line, touching both sides, but mostly in the middle somewhere." — *Maureen Reddy,* Crossing the Color Line

Even at this very moment vision moves backward and forward, challenging who I think I am. There is no final resting place until that final rest, and would you rather be dead? I ask myself when I feel unhinged by psychic vertigo, usually in the middle of the night but sometimes walking down some bright, daylight street as well. The image of a fabric has come to me repeatedly all through this memoir, many threads woven into a pattern which might be rewoven at another time. A self-portrait as common as if it were made of unbleached cotton wool, not only the moments of being but also the ordinary materials of daily life.

It is Christmas 1994. Khary has been in Kingston, Jamaica for four months, studying African Caribbean literature and history at the University of West Indies during the fall semester of his senior year at college. Adam, who has been living and working as an actor in Hollywood for the past two years, is coming home for the holidays. They are both arriving at Kennedy Airport on the same night.

Adam's plane arrives first and while Douglas drives around the airport, unable to park at this time of year, I go to find him in the crowded terminal. He comes down the ramp but doesn't see me, so for a moment I have the rare luxury of watching him, unseen. I remember viewing him surreptitiously like this when he was a child playing in his room during one of his unusual moments of solitude. He was an extremely social child, always seeking connection. He talked so much and so fast sometimes I thought I'd be brought to tears, partly because he always demanded a response, some expressed sign of indisputable interest. I remember noticing how Lois would often pretend to listen to family members who incessantly sought her attention, while also maintaining a kind of mental solitude amidst the noise by saying a casual, regular, mmm, hmm, punctuating someone else's soliloquy. One day, walking Adam to school, I tried Lois's ploy on him. Mmm, hmm, I said offhandedly when he asked me a question following a long monologue. "Don't say mmm, hmm to me," he said angrily. "I want you to really answer me and look at me right in the eyes when you do."

His dark hair is streaked with premature white, like my father's was. A tall, handsome Black man who obviously has some kind of mixed gene pool in his origins. As usual, he appears wide-eyed, his face open to the world. A few stares follow us as we move toward each other into a tight embrace. I feel them on my skin, on his, but they disappear from my consciousness the moment we begin to talk — Here you are at last! — Did you check any bags? — Where's Dad? — I have to pee — What time does Khary's plane come in?

It is an hour later than scheduled when it does, and then we wait another hour and a half while the passengers go through customs behind closed doors, emerging in a slow stream, about one every five minutes, each pushing a supermarket cart full of luggage. We are surrounded mostly by Jamaicans waiting for relatives, some of them patiently, like Adam and Douglas, some of them impatiently like me. A tall, angular, middle-aged man who is waiting next to me suddenly explodes, "Are they mad! Will they never come out?!"

The waiting room is getting emptier and emptier. I try to glimpse behind the swinging doors as other passengers emerge, seeing if I can spot my son. Then finally he is there, walking toward us behind his shopping cart which is filled with a huge brown basket and the old green duffle bag he once took to camp, now stuffed with dirty laundry, pieces of which are falling out into the cart. His skin, darkened by his four months in the sun, shines beneath his long brown curls. His beard is shorter than when he left but he seems the same, no newly born "Rasta Man" a Jamaican friend warned us would probably return.

"They had me waiting all this time while they went through every single piece of dirty clothes, through the pages of every single one of my books. They think I'm a drug dealer, of course. I just sat there laughing at them," he is saying to his father and brother as I walk up to them and take him for a long, long moment into my arms.

As we move down the Van Wyck Expressway from the airport in Queens toward Manhattan, I feel Khary's joy at returning to his city, the only geographical place that he can call home. "When people ask me where I am from," he wrote to us in a letter from Jamaica, "I can only bring myself to say, New York City. In America, I stand on the outside, and there are everyday reminders that America does not consider me one of its own. A place that rejects you cannot be home."

As often happens to me these days, words of James Baldwin come to mind:

"This world is white no longer, and it will never be white again."[1]

I read this extraordinary sentence from "Stranger in the Village," written by Baldwin in 1953, as a statement of a reality as undeniable and obvious as the passage of time. It is certainly a statement about power, but also an interrogation of the very concept of whiteness. It is the theme upon which everything I have written is a variation. Where does this knowledge leave an ex-white person?

I have been born into color. But what is the name of this color, and what are its social conditions and requirements, its layers beneath the skin? To begin to respond to this question I ask myself another: what do I know in other circumstances of being born?

When I began to write seriously — that is, in a disciplined way — when I was born, in other words, into being a writer, I also had just had a child. I thought I had nothing to write about because motherhood represented only something personal, not potentially transformative or transcendent, certainly not literary. It was a revelation to read writers such as Tillie Olsen who was using her knowledge of motherhood as metaphoric, enabling her to write of many layers of human experience. I have written many different stories since that revelation, but being a mother continued to be a central passion of my life, and so it was one of the experiences I most wanted to write about, for the same reasons any writer wants to write about her passions — to name them more accurately, to understand them, to convey meaning to others, to use one's own life to think about life itself.

But putting the mother's voice into literature involved breaking an old and ingrained polarity. One side of the polarity says that motherhood *is* life — an isolating experience yet one which dwarfs all others; that once I become a mother that is fundamentally what I am. The opposite view is that motherhood is not real life at all, but an adjunctive experience for an independent woman doing serious things. Serious things involve moral, political, aesthetic, intellectual engagement, while motherhood is not so much a way of seeing as a particular set of blinders which keep one from seeing clearly at all.

The philosopher Sara Ruddick, in her ground-breaking book, *Maternal Thinking,* demystifies the experience in part by writing of motherhood as a discipline, a development of knowledge and skill over time which includes leaps and regressions, achievements and failures, transcendence and limits, much like any other discipline seriously undertaken.[2] The initial engagement comes from inspiration and passion. But in no discipline are these enough. They must be balanced by thought and action which are often contrary to one's desires, and by devotion, which the thesaurus associates with both attention and resolution, and which provides energy when passion is spent. Thought, action, and devotion do not always come naturally. One engages in them, in part and at times, because one believes one must, not always because at every moment desire spurs one on.

All the preoccupying signs of even small, daily rebirths have been with me for days. I forget my words in meetings and even in my classroom. Strange mistakes instead of coherent sentences erupt from my mouth. Yesterday, in my class in autobiographical fiction, I called one of my students by the name of her character in her fiction, after nearly an entire semester of insisting on the crucial and mysterious space between the writer and her creation, no matter how closely that character is based upon herself. Next, I looked straight into the face of one of the most active students in the class, a woman I know well, and said, Where is Zelda? I haven't seen her yet — referring to the student whose face I was looking into. Later, during a meeting about teaching writing to freshmen, I kept losing my words, before them my thoughts. But it was not as if I were preoccupied with other thoughts. Rather, I felt blank inside, empty of language, filled with presences that can be called neither thought nor feeling, nothing so exact, but rather a sense of fullness without shape, of being blown up beyond my usual contours with something that feels familiar and important yet unknown and unnamed.

I write that sentence as the thought comes to me, not planning a metaphor. Only at the end of the sentence do I realize I am describing pregnancy.

I feel the mixture of being completely lost and completely home I remember from my first pregnancy in 1968.

Being born into a consciousness of color is to be born into color. Being born means willfully engaging the discipline ahead — the development of knowledge over time.

There is a great false myth that while we create our children, they merely react to us, as if we were static creatures, finished and formed. The truth is more reciprocal. Like any passionate intimacy, they (re)create us at the same moment as we are creating and recreating them.

Everywhere mothers are told we have nothing left to offer grown children, especially sons, except our permission for them to separate, respect for their boundaries, a kind of distanced noninterference while keeping our feelings and thoughts to ourselves. Like the myths of early motherhood which depict new mothers as full of instantaneous love and instinctual selflessness, this popular and professional wisdom about mothering grown-ups is a distortion because it is only half the story. Certainly my sons are separate adults engaged in creating their own lives which often have little to do with me. But in my life and in my dreams they remain sources of cherished and immutable attachment, influencing me as I influence them.

If love is the theme, then devotion is a variation which, like a riff by Coltrane, can sometimes evoke dissonance and pain.

Lights are moving swiftly by me as I look out the car window to my left while Khary sits on my right, holding my hand. It has been painful being apart from him for so long, yet I can already see from a certain way he holds his chin and the tone of a few initial comments that he has been through great changes, is returning to us from what has been an important experience in his life. Threads of the fabric of my life are coming together, finding a pattern which at times will hold.

I am thinking about the balance between the separation of the self and its relation to others, a question which has obsessed me as a writer, which I have named and specified through my experiece as a mother, and which has a special and particular meaning when, as a white American writer, I think about race.

Sometimes when something new is being born there is a sense of convergence, as if writers and thinkers from various places and times were waiting for you to find their words, inviting you into a tradition.

Here are the words of Nadine Gordimer, written out of another racist society, during a time she calls an "interregnum" — a period when something is dying and something else is struggling to be born:

"There are two absolutes in my life. One is that racism is evil—human damnation in the Old Testament sense, and no compromises, as well as sacrifices, should be too great in the fight against it. The other is that a writer is a being in whose sensibility is fused what Lukács calls 'the duality of inwardness and outside world', and he must never be asked to sunder this union."[3]

I return to Achebe's essay on truth and fiction, this time focusing on his last sentences:

"It's truth [the truth of imaginative literature] is not like the canons of an orthodoxy or the irrationality of prejudice or superstition. It begins as an adventure in self-discovery and ends in wisdom and humane conscience."[4]

So fundamental to the experience of motherhood, this relationship between self-exploration and conscience is also the very heart of autobiography for me.

Then I find these words, written by the young Black writer Lisa Jones, about her Jewish mother, Hettie Jones:

"[s]he has taken to checking 'other' on her census form. In the line slotted for explanation she writes, in her flowery longhand, 'Semitic American mother of black children.'"[5]

I gather the two memoirs of mother, *How I Became Hettie Jones,* and daughter, *Tales of Race, Sex and Hair,* from their different shelves and place them next to each other over my desk.

I feel a certain envy of people (including my sons) who have found a solid sense of self and direction in cultural identity, but it is a reality of my situation that I am not grounded in an identity signaled by nationality, color, or religion. We are living in a time when for important historical reasons many are concerned with difference, with not prematurely homogenizing differences or worse, hypocritically denying them in order to remain dominant in one's own difference. Many who speak and write publicly, now, find their identities, their reconstructed selves, in cultural roots.

But this is not where I have found myself.

In trying to map this mobile, protean terrain, I sometimes think of my father who was a member of the Abraham Lincoln Brigade, the American volunteers who went to Spain to fight Franco's fascism. I was proud of that history and deeply affected by it. The position of outsider in American society seemed a moral place to stand. The idea that Spanish fascism was the business of my father, a Russian-born American Jew, seemed unquestionable and right.

Then, recently, I read of an old Creole saying:

> Tell me
> Whom you love, and
> I'll tell
> You who you are.[6]

Baldwin once described the consequences of the daily assaults of racism as: "some dread, chronic disease, the unfailing symptom of which is a kind of blind fever . . . one has the choice, merely, of living with it consciously or surrendering to it."[7]

For him, as for many African Americans, that fever is rage, a never-ending threat of conflict, the daily expectation of intentional and blind injustice. For those of us who are white and count ourselves "progressives" the "fever" may be something else having to do with guilt and shame. I believe that active, ongoing engagement in antiracist work at every level of our social and personal lives is the only way to manage such inevitable feelings, the only way to live consciously, without surrendering. *If the theme is devotion, the variation is action. It solos over the repetitions behind it and repeats, repeats.*

In whatever situations or institutions I find myself, I align myself with Black people, a decision which at times involves conflict because, obviously, there are divisions and differences among Black people within any ideology or community. Still, *aligning myself* means being alert at all times to issues of race and racism, to see this issue as of central importance to the meaning and character of any social or political situation, of primary interest in any book I read or work of art I view, never parenthetical or tangential to questions of worth, to the perception of either beauty or truth.

As I continue to study in the expansive and expanding field of African American culture and history, I think back to the Richmond Museum, the slavery exhibit "Before Freedom Came," and of how that exhibit brought back my experience years before in the Holocaust Museum in Jerusalem. An Israeli-American writer friend of mine informs me that the literal translation of the Hebrew *Yad Vashem* is: give a strong and mighty hand to memory. As I come to the end of this story, although at last the loss of American memory is being reconstructed by artists, scholars, activists, and teachers, I feel with the weight of a necessary burden the lies at the center of the "absolute evil of racism" which continue into our own time, controling our politics, disrupting our society, disturbing our peace — a disturbance which may signify our only possible source of redemption. We cannot erase centuries of slavery, discrimination, and bigotry, but we can begin the process of respectful, truthful remembering. For what sort of psychological distortion must take place in us in order "not to know" the reality of this immense subjugation?

The holocaust of American slavery continued for over two hundred years. Yet, there is still no full-scale slavery museum in this country. It is not only scholars of history who have access to "the world the slaves made." There are narratives, letters, diaries, new books available every year to any American who seeks to know the truth of our history and thus our current life. The alternative is to remain blind to what Toni Morrison has called "a disrupting darkness before [our] eyes."[8]

I have just learned something new about those stones Jews place on the edge of the gravestones of their loved ones. More than the general need to remember, they symbolize the willingness to be a witness. Each stone is a sign that I, the visitor, bear witness to the life that is over, and that as long as I live, I remain a witness to that life, re/membering it (preventing it from losing its wholeness, its coherence, from being *dis/membered*), and thus preserving it.

What does it mean to be a witness to a life, even one's own? What pride or hubris, what *chutzpah* is necessary to attempt such a thing?

Witnessing certainly presupposes the willingness to speak aloud, but there are moments when I feel frightened about publishing this story about the education of one American woman. Writing about my family, checking and rechecking thoughts with them, I nevertheless know this is still only my story. A personal confession is perhaps the essential individual action, contained by one's own perspective, driven by one's own need to make a bridge between solitude and the world.

But I needn't worry, for Adam has just finished a film script about a young Black man falling in love with a Jewish woman while negotiating the powerful forces of racism and misogyny on a college campus in the late 1980s. And on Christmas morning I am presented with an unexpected present from Khary, a novel he has completed while in Jamaica about a young Black man coming of age in New York City, crossing and recrossing the borders between the security of home and the violent streets of the city, always accompanied by a pulsing drumbeat of voices, both destructive and redemptive, in a spiritual realm where he spends much of his time.[9]

Over the next week, we are all trading manuscripts among ourselves and with Douglas, posing questions, offering critique, receiving praise, amazed at the variety of forms and voices, the repetitions and innovations of tone and rhythm that can be generated in one family.

There are still times when I feel intimidated and wary when I bring up the issue of race in large meetings or groups. I may be seen as intrusive by Black friends and colleagues, or as posturing and trying to be "the good white person" by whites. Then, there is solace in remembering Khary's novel, Adam's screenplay, the absolute certainty of voices different from one's own. I step out of the spotlight and see it is less important what either Black or white people think of my comments than that — colored/colorless for a moment — I assert what I believe to be true. This is what I was taught as a child and what I still believe. You speak out against even the smallest injustice, whoever you are, especially if you are in a position of privilege, especially when the injustice is not directed, for the moment perhaps, at you.

You don't have to be Black to realize that African and African American thought and experience is essential for all people to learn if we want to understand the truth of what happened to this world over the last few centuries, truths which landed us in the violent and truly alarming times in which we find ourselves today.

In all racialized situations, that is to say all situations in which Black people and white people who are not on close, personal terms find themselves together, I am always comforted by this thought: I am no longer white. However I may appear to others, I am a person of color now.

How do I imagine this color in moments of solitude when the mind looks in on itself?

A self-portrait in dyed wool: blue, dusty brown, dark grey, forest green. The wool strands hang separately, their eventual pattern only imagined. And I have set myself this task, of making a tapestry of words, a translation of many impressions into one finally meaningful language, of searching for pattern on the uncertain possibility that there is pattern to be found. Every few blues there will be a grey. Every four greys, a deep red. But the pattern is visible only for a moment and then, as it was intended to do, it assumes a collective identity again. A tweed — a greyish, brownish, bluish tweed. Some color with no precise name.

If I were asked to make a wish for my children's adult lives, I would hope for a bridge between the transcient, fluid identity I have known and the reliable place of a strong, rooted self. To know each by the sureness of the other, moving from inward recreations back out to something solid and active, then into the uncertainties of an inward journey again. No premature resolution can cover over the discontinuities and contradictions. The ability to remain with such ambivalence and ambiguity of identity is an aspect of art as well as of love.

NOTES

1 *The Richmond Museum of the Confederacy*

1   Virginia Woolf, "A Sketch of the Past," in *Moments of Being* (New York: Harcourt, Brace, Jovanovich, 1976), p. 72.

2   Chinua Achebe, "The Truth of Fiction," in *Hopes and Impediments* (New York: Anchor, 1989), p. 153.

3   *Before Freedom Came, African American Life in the Antebellum South,* exhibit catalog, (Charlottesville: University Press of Virginia and The Richmond Museum of the Confederacy, 1991), p. 62.

4   Ibid.

5   Harriet Jacobs, *Incidents in the Life of a Slave Girl,* ed., Jean Fagan Yellin (Cambridge: Harvard University Press, 1987), p. 77.

6   *Before Freedom Came,* p. 101.

7   Ibid., p. 77.

8   Ibid., p. 61.

9   Ibid., pp. 117, 118.

2 Color Blind: The Whiteness of Whiteness

1 Gary Lemons, "The Blackness of Blackness: Representations of Sexuality in African American Literature," Eugene Lang College Course, n.d.

2 Audre Lorde, "The Transformation of Silence," in *Sister, Outsider* (Trumansberg, N.Y.: The Crossing Press, 1984), p. 42.

3 Adrienne Rich, "Split at the Root," in *Blood, Bread and Poetry, Selected Prose, 1979–1985* (New York: W. W. Norton, 1986), p. 123.

4 Langston Hughes, "Montage of a Dream Deferred," in *The Langston Hughes Reader* (New York: George Braziller Inc., 1958), p. 89.

5 Meridel Le Seuer, "I Was Marching," in *Ripening: Selected Work, 1927–1980* (New York: Feminist Press, 1982).

6 Marlon Williams, unpublished, untitled poem.

7 This is a paraphrased statement made by Primo Levi in a televised documentary that aired on PBS.

8 bell hooks, "Representations of Whiteness," in *Black Looks* (Boston: South End Press, 1992), p. 177.

3 Passing Over

1 Reginald McKnight, "The Kind of Light That Shines on Texas," in *The Kind of Light That Shines on Texas* (Boston: Little, Brown, 1992) p. 37.

2 Sekou Sundiata, *The Circle Is Unbroken Is a Hard Bop,* n.p. (Note: This play is not published but has been performed in various theaters in the United States and Europe.)

3 Adam Lazarre-White, personal correspondence.

4 James Baldwin, "Stranger in the Village," in *The Price of the Ticket* (New York: St. Martins, 1985), p. 81.

5 James Baldwin, *Got Tell It on the Mountain* (New York: Laurel, 1952).

6 Toni Morrison, *The Bluest Eye* (New York: Pocket Books, 1970).

7 Achebe, "The Truth of Fiction," p. 144.

8 Albert Camus, "Create Dangerously," in *Resistance, Rebellion and Death* (New York: Knopf, 1960).

9 James Baldwin, Interview, *New York Times,* January 10, 1985, p. 17 (quoted in his obituary, *New York Times,* December 1, 1987, p. 27).

10 Patricia J. Williams, *The Alchemy of Race and Rights* (Cambridge: Harvard University Press, 1991), p. 235.

11 First published by Eugene Lang College in "Final Report to the Ford Foundation on a Program to Create Diversity throughout the College Community," March 1995.

12 Tillie Olsen, "Silences," in *Silences* (New York: Delta, 1965).

13 Alice Walker, "In Search of Our Mothers' Gardens," in *In Search of Our Mothers' Gardens* (New York: Harvest, 1983).

14 Gloria Hull, Patricia Bell Scott, and Barbara Smith, eds., *All the Women Are White, All the Blacks Are Men, but Some of Us Are Brave.* (Old Westbury, N.Y.: Feminist Press, 1981).

15 Ruth Frankenberg, *The Social Construction of Whiteness,* (Minneapolis: The University of Minnesota Press, 1993), p. 79.

16 Toni Morrison, *Beloved,* (New York: Plume, 1988), p. 89.

17 Frederick Douglass, "Narrative of the Life of Frederick Douglass," in *Classic Slave Narratives,* ed., Henry Louis Gates, Jr. (New York: Mentor, 1987), pp. 294–98.

18 Robin Morgan, "The Network of the Imaginary Mother, Part IV: The Child," in *Upstairs in the Garden, Poems Selected and New, 1968–1988* (New York: W. W. Norton, 1990).

19 Toni Morrison, *Jazz* (New York: Knopf, 1992), p. 173.

20 James Baldwin, "Notes of a Native Son," in *The Price of the Ticket,* pp. 140–41.

21 Rita Dove, "Canary," in *Grace Notes* (New York: W. W. Norton, 1989).

22 hooks, "Representations," p. 177.

23 Houston A. Baker, Jr., *Blues, Ideology and Afro-American Literature* (Chicago: University of Chicago Press, 1984), epigraph.

4 Reunions, Retellings, Refrains

1 John Edgar Wideman, *Fatheralong* (New York: Vintage Books, 1995), p. 109.

2 Wideman, *Fatheralong,* p. 111.

3 Ibid., p. 109.

4 Morrison, *Jazz,* p. 30.

5 Baker, *Blues,* p. 202.

6 Khary Lazarre-White, personal narrative, 1992.

7 1 Cor. 13., King James Version (New York: American Bible Society).

8 Woolf, "A Sketch of the Past," p. 72.

9 Lorde, "The Transformation of Silence," p. 42.

10 Morrison, *Jazz,* p. 99.

11 Khary Lazarre-White, personal narrative, 1992.

5 A Color with No Precise Name

1 Baldwin, "Stranger in the Village," p. 90.

2 Sara Ruddick, *Maternal Thinking* (Boston: Beacon Press, 1989).

3 Nadine Gordimer, "Living in the Interregnum," in *The Essential Gesture* (New York: Knopf, 1988), p. 276.

4 Achebe, "The Truth of Fiction," p. 153.

5 Lisa Jones, "Mama's White," in *Tales of Race, Sex and Hair* (New York: Doubleday, 1994), p. 32.

6 Joe Wood, "Escaping Blackness," quoted in *The Village Voice,* 6 December 1994.

7 Baldwin, "Notes of a Native Son," p. 133.
8 Toni Morrison, *Playing In The Dark* (Cambridge: Harvard University Press, 1990), p. 91.
9 Adam Lazarre-White, "The Other Side of the River"; Khary Lazarre-White, "Blood Witness."

Jane Lazarre is Director of the Writing Program and
Professor of Writing and Literature at Eugene Lang College,
New School for Social Research, New York. She is the
author of *The Mother Knot*, a memoir, the novels *Some Kind
of Innocence*, *The Powers of Charlotte*, and *Worlds Beyond My
Control*, and a volume of essays, *On Loving Men*.

Library of Congress Cataloging-in-Publication Data
Lazarre, Jane.
Beyond the whiteness of whiteness : memoir of a white
mother of black sons / Jane Lazarre.
ISBN 0-8223-1826-1 (cloth : alk. paper)
ISBN 0-8223-2044-4 (pbk. : alk. paper)
1. Mother and sons — United States.   2. Children of
interracial marriage — United States.   I. Title.
HQ755.85.L39   1996
306.874'3 — dc20   96-452 CIP